D1592565

MAKERS
of the
MUSLIM
WORLD

'Abd al-Ghani al-Nabulusi

SELECTION OF TITLES IN THE MAKERS OF
THE MUSLIM WORLD SERIES

Series editor: Patricia Crone,
Institute for Advanced Study, Princeton

For current information and details of other books in the
series, please visit www.oneworld-publications.com

MAKERS
of the
MUSLIM
WORLD

'Abd al-Ghani al-Nabulusi

Islam and the Enlightenment

SAMER AKKACH

ONEWORLD

OXFORD

'ABD AL-GHANI AL-NABULUSI

A Oneworld Book
Published by Oneworld Publications 2007

Copyright © Samer Akkach 2007

ISBN-13: 978–1–85168–508–0

Typeset by Jayvee, Trivandrum, India
Printed and bound in India for Imprint Digital

Oneworld Publications
185 Banbury Road
Oxford OX2 7AR
England
www.oneworld-publications.com

To Salwa, Sami, and Sarmad

with love and gratitude

CONTENTS

PART II HIS THOUGHT: A VIEW FROM WITHOUT

There has arisen in this time a shining planet from the concealment of being's closure, and there has appeared an enlightening full moon from the sky of witnessed disclosure, and there has broken forth an illuminating sun from the presence of the Praised Station.

Al-Baytamani, *al-Mashrab al-Hani*, 4.

PREFACE

Before the wholesale adoption of the European Enlightenment ideas by nineteenth-century Arab and Ottoman intellectuals, Muslim scholars of the seventeenth and eighteenth centuries had their own intellectual program that dictated their exchanges with the West. It influenced the choices they had made and enabled them to deal confidently with the new emerging ideas. In a sense, it can be said that they had their own enlightenment. 'Abd al-Ghani al-Nabulusi (1641–1731) of Damascus, a contemporary of many major thinkers, scientists, poets, and philosophers of the European Enlightenment, was one of the key figures of the Islamic enlightenment. His life and work enable us to trace points of crossing with, and difference from, the European experience. As a leading religious scholar of the time, 'Abd al-Ghani exerted his influence mainly in the domain of religious sciences, to which he made significant contributions.

The European Enlightenment marks an important phase in world intellectual history, one that is recognized for laying the foundations for, and shaping the rational sensibility of, the modern world. One of the key characteristics of the Enlightenment was the changing attitude toward religion, reflected in clashes between faith and reason, religion and science. The growing reverence for science and human reason, as a result of the scientific revolution of the seventeenth century, was associated with increasing irreverence toward religion and the authority of the church. New contrasting trends emerged: along with secularism and growing anti-religious sentiment, fresh religious ideas introduced new understandings of the relationship between God, man, and the world. The period also saw the emergence of new ways of understanding otherness, shifting the vantage point from religion to anthropology. The faith and unbelief polarity was replaced by that of knowledge and ignorance.

In the Islamic world, Islam did not encounter the same level of hostility from rationalists as Christianity did in Europe. Nor was its religious worldview shaken to the core in the same way the Christian worldview was by new scientific findings. But most importantly, otherness continued to be viewed in terms of religion rather than anthropology. This was related, among other things, to the state of science in seventeenth- and eighteenth-century Islam. Notwithstanding the keen attempts to keep up with the latest scientific developments, the intensity of the scientific enterprise of the Muslims never matched that of the Europeans, and reverence for science never reached the heights it did in Europe. Yet, rational trends of thought emerged, finding expression in some secular and scientific writings, in religious reform and anti-mystical sentiment, in an increased sophistication of religious thinking, and in some changes to the modes of production and communication of knowledge.

The multifaceted personality and teachings of 'Abd al-Ghani reflect several aspects of these rational trends. Through his personality, he presented a new individualistic model of a self-made Sufi master, one who relied on texts rather than masters for spiritual attainment, and one who saw no conflict between worldly pleasure and spiritual fulfilment. Through his teachings, he attempted to expand the scope of rationality of religious thinking. He articulated a philosophy of religion that supported an ecumenical and egalitarian understanding of Islam and enhanced its scope of tolerance, and introduced a philosophy of being as a viable alternative to the natural theology that was emerging in Europe. Through his public readings of highly controversial mystical texts, he also strove to create a new social space for mysticism, one that promoted public participation rather than privacy, secrecy, and elitism. His attempt to exploit the power of the public to counter the rising anti-mystical sentiment was unprecedented in Damascus, generating at once much interest and unease.

'Abd al-Ghani's conspicuous affiliation with Sufism is behind his current monochromatic image as a Sufi saint. A Sufi saint though he was, his thought and teachings had much more to them than Sufism. Through a fresh reading of his unpublished biographical sources and large body of mostly unpublished works, this study attempts to construct a more complex and colourful image of 'Abd al-Ghani, one that sheds new light on his hitherto unexplored contributions to the intellectual history of Islam.

ACKNOWLEDGEMENTS

Research for this book was supported by several Faculty Grants from the University of Adelaide and a large Discovery Grant from the Australian Research Council (ARC). I am grateful to both institutions for their generous support. Because of the lack of studies on 'Abd al-Ghani al-Nabulusi and the paucity of his published works, I have had to work with a large body of unpublished material, which I acquired from al-Asad Library in Damascus and the library of Princeton University. I wish to thank the Director General of al-Asad Library, 'Ali al-'Aidi, and the Head of the Manuscripts Section, Farouq al-Munajjid, for granting me permission to acquire copies of many of al-Nabulusi's unpublished works, and for facilitating my study during several visits. Special thanks are also due to the staff of the Manuscripts and Photocopy Sections for their unfailing assistance and support, and to the Head of the Cultural Section, Mazen 'Arafe, for his insight, intellectual exchange, and keen interest in my work. I wish to thank shaykh Ratib al-Nabulusi and shaykh Adib al-Nabulusi, both descendants of shaykh 'Abd al-Ghani al-Nabulusi, for their valuable guidance and support, AnnaLee Pauls from Princeton University Library for her assistance in acquiring copies of Arabic manuscripts by and on al-Nabulusi, Selen Morkoc for her dedicated research work that uncovered key Ottoman sources on the history of science, and Mehtap Serim for her hospitality and generous help in locating and acquiring several of those valuable sources. Without Mehtap's much appreciated guidance, I would not have been able to find my way around the various libraries in Istanbul. I also would like to thank the staff in the Kandilli Observatory Library, the Topkapi Saray Library, the Süleymaniye Library, and 'Atif Effendi Library, for their help and support, with special thanks to the Director of the Süleymaniye Library, Nevzat Kaya, for his kind and generous help in locating and reproducing a key Ottoman source. I wish to extend my thanks to the series editor, Patricia Crone, for her patient readings and insightful criticism of the first drafts that resulted in substantial improvements, to Sam Ridgway for commenting on parts of the early drafts, to Ahmad Shboul and Nijmeh Hajjar for their valuable feedback and suggestions, and to all the wonderful friends and colleagues in Istanbul and Damascus who never fail to make my visits delightfully memorable.

GLOSSARY

Ash'ari: A follower of al-Ash'ariyya, the theological school founded by Abu al-Hasan al-Ash'ari (d. 935–6) in response to the rational theology advocated by a group known as Mu'tazila. It has since been the predominant theological school among ortho-dox Muslims.

Fada'il: Plural of *fadila*, "virtue," "merit," or "excellence." It desig-nates a genre of historical writing concerned with the virtues of certain towns, times, texts, and individuals based on the Qur'an and prophetic sayings. The most common are texts concerned with the virtues of cities and places that present a form of Islamic sacred history of geography and human settlements.

Fatwa: A "legal opinion" according to the Islamic law normally issued by a jurisconsult, a jurist, or a cleric well-versed in Islamic law.

Fiqh: Literally, "understanding" or "knowing." It is the technical term for "jurisprudence" in the Islamic sciences of religious law. *Faqih* (pl. *fuqaha*'), "jurist," is one who professes or practices the science of Islamic law.

Hadith: Literally, "speech," "saying," and "talk." In Islamic religious sciences, it refers to the reported sayings of the Prophet Muhammad. *'Ilm al-hadith* is the "science of prophetic traditions" that deals with the authentication of the reported accounts of what the Prophet said or did.

Hanafi: One of the four schools of Islamic law; the other three being the Shafi'i, the Maliki, and the Hanbali. It also refers to a follower of this school. It was the official school of the Ottomans.

Haqiqa: Literally, "truth" or "reality," from *haqq*, the "Real," one of God's ninety-nine most beautiful names identified in the Qur'an.

It is commonly used in mystical writing in contrast to *shari'a*, "divine law."

Mufti: "Jurisconsult," one who is officially appointed to give legal advice and issue legal opinions according to the Islamic law.

Murid: A novice "seeker" on the mystical path; from the Arabic roots *arada*, "to will," and *irada*, "will." It designates the "seeker" as one with will and determination to reach one's spiritual goals.

Qibla: The direction Muslims face in their daily pray. First, it was the direction of Jerusalem but was then changed to Mecca.

Shafi'i: One of the four schools of Islamic law; the other three being the Hanafi, the Maliki, and the Hanbali. It also refers to a follower of this school.

Shari'a: Literally, "law;" in the Islamic context, "divine law." It is the system of rules, injunctions, and prohibitions that is derived from the Qur'an and the Prophetic traditions.

Shi'i: A follower of the *shi'a* sect that emerged in the formative period of Islam after a political dispute involving 'Ali, the Prophet's son-in-law. The *shi'a* is the dominant sect in Iran.

Sunni: A follower of the *sunna*, the Prophet's way of life that came to represent orthodox Islam. The *sunnis*, the orthodox Muslims, are the dominant sect in Islam.

Sufi: "Mystic," a follower of the mystical path. Historically, Sufis have had an uneasy relationship with mainstream Islam.

Tariqa: Literally, "way" or "technique;" in mystical literature, the "pathway" of spirituality, a corollary of *haqiqa*, "truth," the destination of the spiritual journey.

Ulama: Literally, "those who know." It is used to identify both religious authorities and scientists, since the root *'ilm* in Arabic means "science" and "knowledge." In premodern Islam it referred specifically to the "jurists," a powerful group of clerics that represented religious authority.

ABBREVIATIONS

For ease of identifying the primary Arabic sources cited in the study the following abbreviations of titles are used. MS identifies unpublished texts.

Ajwiba	*Al-Ajwiba 'ala Wahid wa Sittun Su'al* (al-Nabulusi)
'Aqa'id	*Risala fi al-'Aqa'id al-Islamiyya* (al-Nabulusi, MS)
Bawatin	*Bawatin al-Qur'an wa Mawatin al-Furqan* (al-Nabulusi, MS)
Bayan	*Kashf al-Bayan 'an Asrar al-Adyan* (al-Nabulusi, MS)
Burhan	*Burhan al-Thubut fi Tabri'at Harut wa Marut* (al-Nabulusi, MS)
Dhakha'ir	*Dhakha'ir al-Mawarith fi al-Dalala 'ala Mawadi' al-Ahadith* (al-Nabulusi)
Diwan	*Diwan al-Haqa'iq wa Majmu' al-Raqa'iq* (al-Nabulusi)
EI²	*Encyclopaedia of Islam*, 2nd edition.
Fath	*Al-Fath al-Rabbani wa al-Fayd al-Rahmani* (al-Nabulusi)
Fusus	*Fusus al-Hikam* (Ibn 'Arabi)
Hadiqa	*Al-Hadiqa al-Nadiyya Sharh al-Tariqa al-Muhammadiyya* (al-Nabulusi, MS)
Hadra	*Al-Hadra al-Unsiyya fi al-Rihla al-Qudsiyya* (al-Nabulusi)
Han	*Khamrat al-Han wa Rannat al-Alhan* (al-Nabulusi)
Haqiqa	*Al-Haqiqa wa al-Majaz fi Rihalt Bilad al-Sham wa Misr wa al-Hijaz* (al-Nabulusi)
Hayakil	*Hayakil al-Nur* (al-Suhrawardi)
Insan	*Risala fi Haqiqat al-Insan* (Kemal Pashazade, MS)
Jahil	*Radd al-Jahil ila al-Sawab fi Jawaz Idafat al-Ta'thir ila al-Asbab* (al-Nabulusi, MS)
Jawab	*al-Jawab 'ala Su'al Warad min Taraf al-Nasara* (al-Nabulusi, MS)
Jawahir	*Jawahir al-Nusus fi Hall Kalimat al-Fusus* (al-Nabulusi, MS)

Kashf	*Kashf al-Zunun 'an Asami al-Kutub wa al-Funun* (Hajji Khalifa)
Kawakib	*Al-Kawakib al-Sa'ira bi-A'yan al-Ma'a al-'Ashira* (al-Ghazzi)
Kawkab	*Al-Kawkab al-Mutalali fi Sharh Qasidat al-Ghazali* (al-Nabulusi, MS)
Khamrat	*Khamrat Babel wa Shaduw al-Balabel* (al-Nabulusi)
Khulasat	*Khulasat al-Athar fi A'yan al-Qarn al-Hadi 'Ashar* (al-Muhibbi)
Lu'lu'	*Al-Lu'lu' al-Maknun fi Hukm al-Ikhbar 'amma Sayakun* (al-Nabulusi)
Ma'iyya	*Miftah al-Ma'iyya fi Tariq al-Naqshbandiyya* (al-Nabulusi, MS)
Mashrab	*Al-Mashrab al-Hani fi Tarjamat al-'Arif Sidi 'Abd al-Ghani* (al-Baytamani, MS)
Matin	*Al-Radd al-Matin 'ala Muntaqis al-'Arif Muhyi al-Din* (al-Nabulusi, MS)
Mawakib	*Al-Mawakib Al-Islamiyya fi al-Mamalik wa al-Mahasin al-Shamiyya* (Ibn Kinnan al-Salihi)
Miftah	*Miftah al-Futuh fi Mishkat al-Jism wa Zujajat al-Nafs wa Misbah al-Ruh* (al-Nabulusi, MS)
Milal	*Al-Milal wa al-Nihal* (al-Shahrastani)
Muftari	*Radd al-Muftari 'an al-Ta'n bi al-Shushtari* (al-Nabulusi, MS)
Munajat	*Munajat al-Hakim wa Munaghat al-Qadim* (al-Nabulusi, MS)
Mustasfa	*Al-Mustasfa min 'Ilm al-Usul* (al-Ghazali)
Nafahat	*Nafahat al-'Azhar 'ala Nasamat al-Ashar* (al-Nabulusi)
Qala'id	*Al-Qala'id al-Jawhariyya fi Tarikh al-Salihiyya* (Ibn Tulun)
Radd	*Al-Radd 'ala man Takallam fi Ibn al-'Arabi* (al-Nabulusi, MS)
Shajara	*Al-Shajara al-Nu'maniyya al-Kubra fi al-Dawla al-'Uthmaniyya wa ma Yata'allaq bi-Muddatiha min al-Hawadith al-Kawniyya* (Ibn 'Arabi, MS)
Shawakil	*Shawakil al-Hur fi Sharh Hayakil al-Nur* (al-Dawani)
Ta'nif	*Radd al-Ta'nif 'ala al-Mu'annif wa Ithbat Jahl haza al-Musannif* (al-Nabulusi, MS)
Tahrik	*Tahrik Silsilat al-Widad fi Mas'alat Khalq Af'al al-'Ibad* (al-Nabulusi, MS)

Takmil	*Takmil al-Nu'ut fi Luzum al-Buyut* (al-Nabulusi, MS)
Tari	*Al-Fath al-Tari al-Jani fi ba'd Ma'athir 'Abd al-Ghani* (al-Siddiqi, MS)
Tarjuman	*Tarjuman al-Ashwaq* (Ibn 'Arabi)
Ta'tir	*Ta'tir al-Anam fi Ta'bir al-Manam* (al-Nabulusi)
Tuhfat	*Tuhfat al-Udaba' wa Salwat al-Ghuraba'* (al-Khiyari)
'Ulum	*Miftah al-Sa'ada wa Misbah al-Siyada fi Maudu'at al-'Ulum* (Tashkubrizade)
'Uzr	*'Uzr al-A'imma fi Nush al-Umma* (al-Nabulusi, MS)
Wird	*Al-Wird al-Unsi wa al-Warid al-Qudsi fi Tarjamat al-Shaykh 'Abd al-Ghani al-Nabulusi* (al-Ghazzi, MS)
Wujud	*Al-Wujud al-Haqq wa al-Khitab al-Sidqq* (al-Nabulusi)

ILLUSTRATIONS

INTRODUCTION

In the history of the Arab peoples, the transition into modernity is commonly known to have been prompted by the intense interactions with Europe that occurred in the nineteenth century. During this period, a host of influential Arab thinkers were exposed to European ideas while the Europeans had an expanding colonial presence in the Arab world that began with the French invasion of Egypt in 1798. At the turn of the nineteenth century, most of the Arabic-speaking world was under the waning control of the Turks, who were well aware of the ailing state of their empire. Despite their aversion toward the rising power of Europe, both Arab and Turkish intellectuals were fascinated by the intellectual developments and scientific achievements of the Europeans. In their attempts to remedy the state of decline they found themselves in, they espoused the ideas that emerged in Europe in the eighteenth century, the period commonly known as the Enlightenment, and embarked upon a wide-scale program of reform. The main aim of the program was to catch up with the advances of the Europeans that resulted in the new, progressive, and liberal modes of living and thinking that were then perceived as "modern." Influenced by the intellectual orientations of the European Enlightenment, so named to celebrate the shining light of human reason and triumph of science over religion, nineteenth-century Arab intellectuals saw the preceding period, the seventeenth and eighteenth centuries, as one of unenlightenment and held it responsible for their state of backwardness. In the manner of the Enlightenment thinkers, they upheld their program of reform as one of awakening, and like the enlightened Europeans, the awakened Arabs sharply distinguished their vanguard, rational efforts from the ignorance and oblivion of the preceding generations, emphasizing the intellectual discontinuity with their ideas. Their views prevailed among the Arabs, who have since had a dismissive attitude toward the closing chapter of their pre-modernity.

This study of 'Abd al-Ghani al-Nabulusi's life and works shifts the focus back onto this disowned chapter in the intellectual history of the Arabs in the Middle East. It uses 'Abd al-Ghani as a lens to view the intellectual developments in the pre-awakening period that were concurrent with the scientific revolution and the Enlightenment in Europe. It focuses on the relationship between science and religion and the early expressions of rationalism among Arab and Turkish scholars. The confrontation between science and religion in Europe was one of the most important developments of this period, resulting in the divergence of the scientific and religious worldviews, in the spread of secularism, and the rise of anti-religious sentiment. This is used as a background against which the intellectual scenes in the Middle East are constructed and within which 'Abd al-Ghani's contributions are located and discussed. The intent is not to trace the circulation of ideas and threads of influences across both the Islamic and Christian worlds, but rather to detect moments of resonance and to identify points of crossing and difference in the European and Islamic experiences. This enables the presentation and discussion of 'Abd al-Ghani's thought in a comparative perspective and allows the appreciation of his contributions in a broader intellectual context.

Before the awakening, the study argues, Muslim scholars (Arabs and Turks) were, to some extent, familiar with the changes that were taking place in Europe. They showed interest in the scientific developments, translated several works on astronomy and geography, and attempted to widen the rational scope of the Islamic faith. Their exchanges with Europe, however, were dictated by the orientation of their intellectual program that rendered them more guarded and selective than their modernist successors. Viewing the Enlightenment broadly as representing a particular way of reasoning about God, man, and the world, contemporary Muslim scholars can be said to have their own distinct way of reasoning. In their search for enlightenment, the

Europeans celebrated the light of human reason and the merit of scientific rationalism. By contrast, contemporary Muslim scholars sought enlightenment through tradition. It is in this sense that they are presented here as having their own enlightenment and not in the sense of sharing the European approach. While thinking in both the Christian and Islamic contexts became more rational and methodical during this period, Muslim thinkers never shared the enlightened Christians' irreverence toward religion and their contempt for tradition. Thus Islamic rationalism and secularism, upon which Islamic modernity was to be based, maintained their own peculiarities that rendered them distinct from the European examples.

The notion of "Islamic enlightenment" is problematic and its merits have already been debated by several scholars (Schulze, 1996; Gran, 1998; Hagen and Seidensticker, 1998; Radtke, 2000). By invoking it here, the intent is not to buy into the debate in support of the notion. The field is still much under-researched for any cogent argument, for or against such notion, to be constructed. Rather, the intent is to highlight the distinction between two modes of engagement with the ideas and precepts of the European Enlightenment, in the awakening and pre-awakening periods, thereby offering an alternative perspective on the roots of modernity in the Arab-Ottoman world.

From the second half of the seventeenth century onward, scholars, scientists, and bureaucrats, Arabs and Turks, were becoming increasingly aware of losing the edge against the advanced Europeans. They nevertheless maintained faith in their ways of reasoning and the merit of their religion-focused intellectual program. Suspicious of the ideas that were coming from the European infidels, they did not attempt to adopt their new methods of thinking, and were able to sustain their traditional curricula and teaching method well into the nineteenth century.

By contrast, the awakened intellectuals of the nineteenth century, having consciously severed their intellectual ties with the preceding generations, were left without an integral intellectual program of their own but only with a mixed bag of often incoherent thoughts and principles that could not withstand the forceful infiltration and wholesale adoption of the European ideas. Awakened though they might have been, the Muslim liberal thinkers of the nineteenth century were confused about how to deal with their tradition. The awakening experience, as inspired by the European Enlightenment, had presented them with the complex problem of tradition and modernity.

UNRESOLVED DILEMMA

The remarkable success achieved in the field of science in Europe in the seventeenth century prompted an unprecedented emphasis on the autonomy of human reason and a rejection of the habitual reliance on religious sources and the authority of tradition. Many European thinkers of the eighteenth century were explicit about their contempt for tradition. They were keen to articulate a distinctly "modern" worldview that followed the dictates of science and reason, which they distinguished from the "traditional" worldview that followed the dictates of faith and religion. They saw the "modern" as something contemporary and new, full of exciting novelties that stood in contrast to the dull and unenlightened traditions of the past. There was a shared desire among many enlightened thinkers for a decisive break with tradition and a conscious rejection of the inheritance of the past. This marked a moment of disjunction between two ways of living and thinking, whereat "tradition" ceased to be the only way of being, transformed into a worldview, and stood in opposition to the "modern." The Europeans also constructed the idea of the "modern" as a universal worldview, the validity of which did not depend on the internal logic of any tradition but on the universality of science and rational thinking. They presented it as a medium of liberation from the constraints of tradition. Thus conceived, the concept of "modernity" earned the enmity of traditionalists, yet its ideals proved to have a universal appeal. Not only had the awakened Arabs and Turks rushed to embrace them but so had the rest of the world.

Notwithstanding the efforts of the awakened intellectuals to modernise the Arab world, such a decisive break with tradition did not occur. Having been awakened from, as it were, a recent nightmare, nineteenth-century intellectuals dismissed only the unenlightened approaches of their immediate predecessors, while romanticizing the achievements of the earlier periods of the Prophet and the golden era. Thus, their relationship to the heritage of the past remained ambivalent: only the recent past was rejected while the distant past was celebrated. Although interest in the distant past (the classical tradition) was common in eighteenth-century Europe, the science-inspired rationalists defined their position on religion and tradition in general and not with reference to a particular period. As there was no decisive discontinuity with tradition in the experience of the Arabs, the intellectual zone separating the modern from the pre-modern has since remained blurred.

In the pre-awakening period, while rationalistic tendencies emerged, tradition and religion were never seriously challenged; there was no discontinuity with tradition and no unsettling dichotomy between the old and the new as was the case in the awakening period. Yet, the perennial debate over the ancient versus the contemporary and over the preference often accorded to the early Muslims was evident, as the following citation by an eminent scholar of the period, Hajji Khalifa (1609–1657), indicates:

Tell those who disregard the merit of the contemporary,
  giving precedence to the early generations.
That that old was once modern,
  and that this modern will in turn become old (*Kashf*, 1:92).

The concept of "modern" referred to here was not yet identified with Europe but rather with the new approaches of the Muslims at the time. These new approaches were not seen to be in opposition to the old ones but sufficiently different to be identified as modern without undermining the continuity of tradition. Thus, the study of the intellectual developments of this period enables us to distinguish between two phases in the transition into modernity: the awakening phase and the pre-awakening phase. The attitude of the Arab scholars toward religion and tradition differed in each phase, and in both phases their stance on these issues also differed from that of the Europeans.

APPROACH

'Abd al-Ghani's life and works offer an opportunity to explore the pre-awakening phase of transition into modernity, a period when the merits of the new European ideas were still being tested. It is an under-explored phase, especially at the intellectual level: its key thinkers are yet to be identified and its intellectual trends are yet to be examined. 'Abd al-Ghani himself is only faintly present in the collective memory of modern Muslims. Very little has been written about him and most of his works are still in manuscripts buried in various libraries around the world. For his contemporaries, however, he was a leading literary and religious figure, an influential Sufi master with a wide circle of followers, and a prolific scholar with a commanding presence in many disciplines. According to his personal notes, the disciplines of knowledge to which he had contributed were: mystical knowledge, prophetic traditions, theology, divine law, Qur'an incantation, history, and literature. His long list of over 280 titles, ranging from one-page treatises to multi-volume books, includes theological, exegetical, legal, and literary studies, four travel memoirs, four major anthologies of poetry, scores of mystical texts, a major index of prophetic traditions, a treatise on architecture, a book on agriculture, a volume on dream interpretation, and a large number of commentaries on mystical poems and religious texts. It also includes many responses to, and critiques of, the works of his contemporaries, revealing rigorous intellectual exchanges across the Islamic world.

'Abd al-Ghani's conspicuous affiliation with Sufism is behind his current monochromatic image as a Sufi saint; however, the rich spectrum of his works, his colourful personality, his rather unusual mix between material pleasure and spiritual devotion, his keen interest in literature and poetry, and his mastery of law and prophetic traditions, all suggest a more complex figure. In some aspects of his religious and intellectual output, he can be regarded as a typical figure of the period, yet in others, such as his Sufi training and the scope of his intellectual contributions, he stands out as a unique figure. Considering the rich variety of his contributions, it is not possible to construct a one-sided image of him based on a representative sample, or the most significant, of his works without being reductive.

The only three lengthy studies available on 'Abd al-Ghani focus mainly on the mystical aspects of his works, presenting him as a leading, popular, and visionary Sufi saint (Aladdin, 1985; Von Schlegell, 1997; Sirriyeh, 2005). This study shifts the focus onto the rational aspects of his works in order to reveal the paradoxical yet creative marriage of rationalism and mysticism in his personality. It discusses four dominant themes in his writings—unity of being, truth–law polarity, causality, and human reality—along with his attitude toward texts, his approach to the study of prophetic traditions, his philosophy of religion, and his unprecedented move to expose mystical science in public. Through these topics, the study presents him as a spiritually-inspired rational thinker, an advocate of truth and social justice.

The study is based on the examination of over 150 of 'Abd al-Ghani's works, including all of his major texts. Of these, only thirty or so are published. His thought is discussed within a comparative framework that presents a reading of the intellectual history of Islam against a broad-brush background of the scientific revolution and the Enlightenment. This approach introduces 'Abd al-Ghani in an unconventional way. Here he appears alongside contemporary figures, Arabs and Turks, with whom he had not interacted, and his contributions are discussed with reference to the struggle between science and religion that seems remote to his immediate concerns. The study also raises questions about topics, like cosmology, on which he was largely silent, and compares him with European thinkers and scientists, with whom he seemed to have little in common. Unconventional though it might be, this approach presents him as a central figure in a wide group of scholars and thinkers who had played, each in his own way, an important role in the intellectual development of Islam at a time of unsettling changes.

HIS LIFE

A View from Within

SAINTLY PREDICTIONS

Around the turn of 1641, a group of Damascene women went to visit an eccentric mystic known as shaykh Mahmud (d. 1641), who was residing in a secluded place at the foothill of Qasiyun, the mount that embraces the city, tending the tomb of a celebrated local mystic, Yusuf al-Qamini (d. 1259). Mystics at that period were popular figures venerated for their devotions and spirituality. They played an important social role in the Islamic society as guardians of piety and religious ethics, as sources of wisdom and esoteric knowledge, and as channels of divine blessing and mercy. It was customary to seek the blessing of famous mystics and to offer them, in a charitable spirit, some food and presents. Among the visiting group was a pregnant woman from a notable Damascene family named Zaynab al-Dwayki, the daughter of an eminent Damascene merchant who died in India during one of his trading journeys. Shaykh Mahmud seemed to have been in a bad mood on that day and was displeased by the visit. As the women approached from a distance, he welcomed them with a few stones. The women were taken aback and began to retreat when the shaykh called upon 'Abd al-Ghani's mother to approach on her own. Unsure of whom he meant, as none of them were known by that name, the women called upon the one carrying a cooked chicken to approach. But the shaykh again threw stones at her, crying: "it is not you whom I meant; I meant 'Abd al-Ghani's mother." Baffled, they turned to the pregnant woman and said: "it seems to be you whom the shaykh meant; go to him." Zaynab approached reluctantly, but much to her surprise the cranky shaykh received her warmly, explaining that he called her "'Abd al-Ghani's mother" because she was carrying 'Abd al-Ghani. He sat her down beside him, generously offered her from the little he had of food and drink, and gave her a silver coin, saying: "give this to 'Abd al-Ghani when he is born." He instructed her to bring the boy to him upon his birth. But the aged shaykh was not destined to see the boy as he died one day before his birth (*Wird*, 27–28).

On Sunday 17 March 1641 (4 of Dhu al-Hijja, the last month of the Muslim lunar calendar, 1050), Zaynab al-Dwayki gave birth to a baby boy at her parents' place, which was located near the Cotton Market at the heart of old Damascus. The boy's father, the promising young bright scholar Isma'il al-Nabulusi, was away in Cairo studying with the leading Egyptian scholars, so it was easy for the mother to name him 'Abd al-Ghani. In accordance with shaykh Mahmud's instruction, she took the baby to his grave and bathed him thoroughly in its soil. Baptized, as it were, in the soil of mysticism, 'Abd al-Ghani was set on the spiritual path to become a mystic by destiny rather than choice (*Wird*).

This is how the story of 'Abd al-Ghani's birth is remembered in Damascus, thanks largely to his own autobiographical notes and to his lucid biographer and nephew Kamal al-Din al-Ghazzi (d. 1799). Its significance evidently lies in its symbolic meaning rather than its historical truth, pointing to the importance of 'Abd al-Ghani. Shaykh Mahmud, who named him and predicted his future, was to become his guardian. At a critical moment of severe illness, at the brink of death, he was to appear to the young 'Abd al-Ghani, save his life, and help him recover. Not only was shaykh Mahmud said to have predicted the coming of 'Abd al-Ghani, but so too was the great Andalusian mystic Ibn 'Arabi (1165–1240) (*Mashrab*, 12). This is a far more significant prediction, given that it presents the coming of 'Abd al-Ghani as a re-manifestation of Ibn 'Arabi's presence and a reviver of his doctrine. Again, this prediction tends to emphasize that 'Abd al-Ghani's adoption of Ibn 'Arabi as his spiritual master was also by destiny rather than choice.

In the Shadow of Controversy

Whether by destiny or by choice Ibn 'Arabi played a significant role in 'Abd al-Ghani's life, who grew up in the shadow of controversy surrounding the great master. The young 'Abd al-Ghani was inspired by Ibn 'Arabi's ideas, avidly read his work, and defended him vigorously against his critics. As one of the most influential figures in the history of Islam, Ibn 'Arabi's thought and teachings have preoccupied Muslim thinkers for centuries. He had such an imposing presence in the Islamic world that for centuries after his death almost every scholar of note found himself forced to define where he stood in relation to Ibn 'Arabi and his legacy (Knysh, 1999). In about 250 years following his death, over 300 legal opinions were issued by various jurists on the status of his faith and teachings (Yahya, 2001, 20).

Ibn 'Arabi was born in Murcia, Spain, in 1165 and moved as a child with his family to Seville where he received his education. He left Spain for the East in his mid thirties and on his way he went through North Africa, the Hijaz, Palestine, Syria, Iraq, and Anatolia. He finally settled in Damascus, where he died at the age of seventy-eight in 1240 (according to the Islamic calendar, and so are all subsequent references to age) and was buried in al-Salihiyya at the foothills of Qasiyun, in the suburb that was later named after him and carries his name to this day. At Mecca, during the pilgrimage, he met a group of Turks from Qunya and Malatya, befriended their leader Majd al-Din Ishaq, and accompanied him on his way back to Anatolia (today Turkey), where both were invited and hosted by the Sultan of Anatolian Seljuks in Qunya, who showed much interest in Ibn 'Arabi. There, Sadr al-Din al-Qunawi (1207–1274), Majd al-Din's gifted son, attracted Ibn 'Arabi's attention, studied with him, and grew up to be one of his most eminent disciples (*EI²*, Ibn al-'Arabi). Sadr al-Din became one of the most celebrated Turkish mystics, who spread Ibn 'Arabi's teachings among the Turks. He was also the teacher of several eminent mystics, such as 'Afif al-Tilimsani, whose works 'Abd al-Ghani avidly read. After then, Ibn 'Arabi had a favourable presence among the Turks, but his sainthood took on an official status with the rise of the Ottomans and their takeover of Damascus.

The Ottomans

In the seventeenth and eighteenth centuries, most parts of the Arabic-speaking Islamic world was under the rule of the Ottomans. "Ottoman" is the English name for the House of 'Uthman, who first appear in history as one out of many Turkish dynasties controlling Anatolia. They rose to power toward the end of the thirteenth century, first founding a small state on the doorstep of the Byzantines in the north-west of Anatolia, and then expanding rapidly to defeat the Byzantines and take over Anatolia, large parts of the Islamic world, and parts of Europe. In the early phase of their expansion, the Ottomans captured Bursa in 1326 and Adrianople (today Edirne) in 1361; each in turn served as the Empire's capital. By the time they tightened their grip on the Byzantine capital, Constantinople, large parts of the Balkan Peninsula were already under their control. Constantinople fell in 1453 and was soon made the new capital, renamed Istanbul. The Ottomans then moved south. They conquered Damascus and Cairo in 1516–1517, terminating for good the reign of the Mamluks, and took over Baghdad in 1534, which they lost to the Safavids in 1623, only to recapture it in 1638.

The Ottomans conquered in the name of Islam. By the turn of the seventeenth century, Islam had become the official religion of a prosperous civilization extending from Spain to China. It had also taken deep root in south-east Asia and penetrated into western and central Africa. Three imperial powers dominated the vast territories of the Islamic world: the Ottomans, the Safavids, and the Mughals. In their formative periods, the three empires drew their strength from areas inhabited by Turkish tribesmen and their military success was linked to their superior military organization and innovative use of gunpowder. The Ottoman Empire was the largest of the three, in fact, the largest the western part of the world had known since the Roman Empire. It extended over the Middle East, North Africa, Anatolia, and south-eastern Europe. The Safavid Empire, by contrast, was confined to Iran and neighbouring regions, while the Mughal Empire was based in India. The Ottomans ruled over almost all of the Arabic-speaking Muslim countries, except for small pockets, for over 400 years. The Empire reached its zenith during the reign of Sultan Süleyman (1520–1566), who is known in the Arabic-speaking world as Süleyman the Law Maker (al-Qanuni) and in the West as Süleyman the Magnificent.

With the vast territories they controlled, the Ottomans embraced the rich mixture of cultural and political traditions of disparate ethnic groups: Turks, Persians, Mongols, Arabs, and Europeans. The Ottoman state, like other Islamic states, rested on the principle of absolute authority vested in the Sultan, who also held the title of Caliph from the sixteenth century onward. The Ottomans established a central government in Istanbul responsible for maintaining law and order throughout the empire. This complex task involved appointing provincial governors and key officials, collecting taxes, defending and expanding the Empire's frontiers, and ensuring the security of the holy sanctuaries of Mecca and Medina. The official language of the Empire was Turkish but the primary language of learning was Arabic. Arabic was the language of the Qur'an and prophetic traditions, which were the central texts of religious sciences. Most distinguished scholars were trilingual, fluent in Arabic, Turkish and Persian, the main languages of literary production.

Ottoman Damascus

'Abd al-Ghani was born, lived, and died in Ottoman Damascus, the capital of Syria today, where one can still see his grave. Often referred to as al-Sham, Damascus was the largest city in greater Syria, then known as Bilad al-Sham, the region that includes today Syria, Lebanon, Jordan, and Palestine / Israel. Damascus held special significance for early Muslims who considered it a holy city fourth in rank after Mecca, Medina, and Jerusalem. Qur'anic and prophetic references formed the basis of many texts written on its sacred history and religious merits. It was the first Islamic Capital established by the first Muslims outside the Arabian Peninsula in the mid-seventh century, and had remained the seat of government for over ninety years until the centre of power shifted to Baghdad in 750. During the reigns of successive Muslim dynasties, including the Ottomans, Damascus remained an important centre of religious and scientific learning.

The Ottomans conquered Syria and Egypt in 1516–17. After defeating the disorganized Mamluk army near the northern city of Aleppo, Sultan Selim (reigned 1512–1520) had made a peaceful entry into the main cities of Syria. He entered Damascus on 28 September 1516, spent autumn there preparing for the next campaign, and set off with his troops for Egypt at the end of the year. They crossed the Sinai desert with their heavy artillery in five days, humiliated the Mamluks in a single day, killing some 25,000 of them, established Ottoman rule in Cairo, and returned to Damascus ten months later (Shaw, 1976).

Figure 1.1 A Reception of the Venetian Ambassador in late fifteenth-century Damascus, shortly before the Ottoman takeover, by an anonymous Venetian painter (Paris: the Louvre Museum; Howard, 2000, 17).

Sultan Selim showed a special interest in Ibn 'Arabi. Despite his wide reputation and local popularity Ibn 'Arabi's gravesite lay undistinguished in a cemetery at the foothill of Qasiyun for almost three hundred years. Upon his return from Egypt, Sultan Selim commissioned the building of a large complex over his grave, which was designed and constructed with a surprising haste. The Sultan arrived back in Damascus on Wednesday, 21 Ramadan (7 October 1517), the Muslim month of fasting, met with the Governor and local dignitaries, and then immediately commissioned the construction of the complex. On Saturday, the site visit was conducted; on Sunday, an adjacent residence was purchased and a building supervisor was appointed; on Monday, the demolition of existing buildings commenced; and on Tuesday the plans were approved by Sultan Selim himself and the order was issued to commence building. The foundations were dug in the cemetery on Tuesday night to avoid people's anger over the unavoidable disturbance of some of the graves. Sultan Selim spent lavishly on this project and donated generously in celebration of its completion, which he attended before leaving the city. He also set up generous endowments that supported the employment of thirty Qur'an reciters, four announcers of prayer, and a number of teachers, religious leaders, and administrators (Qala'id, 1:114–123).

Sultan Selim's decisive commemoration seems to elevate Ibn 'Arabi overnight to the status of official saint. We do not know the motives behind Sultan Selim's action, but there was in circulation a curious treatise attributed to Ibn 'Arabi together with a commentary by al-Qunawi that predicted the rise of the Ottomans, the conquest of Damascus by Sultan Selim, and the erection of a monument over Ibn 'Arabi's grave. The treatise declared the rise of the Ottomans to be "on the order of God and with the consent of his messenger," and portrayed this major event as an auspicious sign for the prosperity of Islam in the Arab lands (Shajara). Whether this real or fabricated treatise was used to sanction—through the mediation of Ibn 'Arabi's prophecies—the Ottomans' invasion of Damascus and their rule over the rest of the Arabic-speaking Muslim world is uncertain. What is certain, however, is that the transformation of Ibn 'Arabi's humble grave into a significant shrine, signalling the Ottoman endorsement of his sainthood, has played a noticeable role in the development of the city's socio-religious life.

Around the middle of the sixteenth century, Ottoman Damascus was a prosperous and exuberant city with a population of about 55,000—predominantly Sunni Muslims with Christian and Jewish minorities. There were about 7500 Muslim households, 600 Christian, and 520 Jewish. The Rabbi of Ancona, Moses Bassola, one of the earliest European travellers in the Ottoman period, has left a vivid description of the city's social and urban environment:

> Damascus is a great town twice the size of Bologna. It is surrounded by walls and fortifications of great strength and by a moat. There is also a very strong citadel. There are many very beautiful markets, those where trade is carried on being covered on top ... There are to be found all kinds of trades and crafts, to an even greater extent than in Venice. In particular the silk manufacture and trade are on a large scale. Women also earn a lot, and, in general, whoever wishes to exert himself in trade can keep his family there in plenty, even if he has but little capital, for there is profit in everything ... The wealthy acquire large stocks when things are cheap and put them in storage until prices rise ... This land has been blessed with an abundance of foods and fruits and of all kinds of royal dishes and a man can find every kind of pleasure in it ... The houses are beautiful inside with gardens and fountains and in the markets there are fountains in plenty ... They [the Jews] have three synagogues, well built and beautiful, for the Sefardim, one of native Jews of Damascus, and one for Sicilians (Degeorge, 2004, 157).

The mercantile and cosmopolitan character of Damascus intensified in the seventeenth and eighteenth centuries, although most European diplomats were based in the northern city of Aleppo. During this period, according to the Damascene historian Ibn Kinnan (1663–1740), the importance of Damascus also grew over other cities in the province. The unparalleled beauty of its landscape and urban environment, he added, was passionately admired by visitors and locals alike (*Mawakib*, I:197–320). At the turn of the seventeenth century, the French traveller Jacques de Villamont praised the natural beauty and richness with which Damascus was blessed. He wrote: "It is a very large and very powerful city, built on a very beautiful and very rich plain, through which run two rivers ... that subdivide into an infinity of brooks that water delightful gardens ... Whosoever considers the beauty, situation, and richness of this city well would judge it paradise on earth not for the appearance of the city's building, but for the bounty of the land alone" (Degeorge, 2004, 177–178). Several poems by 'Abd al-Ghani corroborate these observations. One opens with the following lines:

> If you are in serious trouble and feeling uneasy,
> > settle in the land of Sham and live in Damascus.
> You will find your desire in it and all that you aspire for,

Figure 1.2 Damascus at the turn of the eighteenth century as depicted by an anonymous European artist. The large building at the centre is the Umayyad great mosque. 'Abd al-Ghani's house was located immediately behind it in the southern direction. The viewer in the painting is facing south (Damascus: 'Azm Palace; Degeorge, 2004, 183).

you will even achieve renown and become eloquent in speech.
A town that rose above all towns in beauty,
   and grew in splendour and increased in glamour ...
If you are to passionately love a home town, this is the one for you,
   above all towns, that deserves to be loved and be enraptured with
(*Khamrat*, 102).

The Ottoman Way

Together with Cairo, Damascus was an important provincial centre
for the Ottomans, especially for the function both served as the
assembly points for the annual pilgrimage caravans heading to
Mecca. Damascus was more important for the Ottomans than Cairo
because it was closer to Istanbul and directly accessible by land. The
pilgrimage to Mecca was one of the most important events on the
Muslim religious calendar, and its organisation involved a considerable amount of effort and resources. Often led by the governor of
Damascus, who carried the title "Prince of the Pilgrimage," accompanied by a special delegate appointed by the Sultan escorting members of the royal family and high officials intending to make the
pilgrimage, the return journey to Mecca took between four and
six months. Ensuring the safe passage of the pilgrims was important
for maintaining stability in the region and for securing the continuous allegiance of the Arab Muslims to the Ottoman Turks.

Sultan Selim made some changes to the governing and legal systems in Damascus to restrict the powers of local officials and judges
and carried out a census for tax purposes. He imposed new taxes that
angered the Damascenes and changed the hierarchy of religious
order that resulted in some confrontations with the Turks. For a long
time, followers of the Shafi'i school of law enjoyed the highest social
status in Damascus, and the chief Shafi'i judge enjoyed special privileges over his fellow judges of the other three schools (Hanafi,
Maliki, and Hanbali). The Ottomans, who adopted the Hanafi law,
changed that order and conferred special privileges onto the Hanafi
religious leaders. When the Shafi'i imam led the congregational

prayer ahead of the Hanafi in the great mosque of Damascus, a scuffle broke out between the Arabs and the Turks and new arrangements had to be agreed. But the Damascenes soon adapted to the new changes and the stability and security provided by the Ottomans led to growth and prosperity.

The Damascenes maintained strong political and cultural ties with Istanbul. As key official appointments were initiated there, Damascene scholars would regularly travel to Istanbul to seek the favours of the Ottomans. Prominent Damascene families were keen to maintain their social prestige and political influence, which depended on their abilities to gain control over various key posts and endowments. Ottoman officials in Istanbul exploited this to maintain control over the province while being careful not to give any local power a chance to acquire a viable threatening edge. They would take account of prestigious genealogy and distinguished scholarly abilities in making their appointments, but unwavering family loyalty to the Ottomans was the decisive criterion. Gaining access to the Ottoman official hierarchy involved the mediation of agents who received payments and gifts. This fostered corruption among Ottoman officials and their Damascene cronies that generated dissent among the locals.

The key posts in Damascus that carried both political clout and religious significance were the principal Preacher (*khatib*) in the Umayyad mosque, the Chief Judge (*qadi al-qudat*), the Chief Jurisconsult (*mufti*), who issued official legal opinions according to the Hanafi law, and Head of descendants of the Prophet Muhammad or Head of the Nobles (*naqib al-ashraf*). These positions were under the control of influential Damascene families: the Bahnasi and the Muhasini families maintained monopoly over the principal Preacher post, the 'Imadi family controlled the Chief Jurisconsult post, and the Hamza and 'Ajlan families monopolized the Head of Nobles post. The Chief Judge post was kept for the Turks (Voll, 1975). These families were highly influential in the Ottoman court and maintaining good relationship with them was important for keeping other less important local posts.

A FAMILY WITH ONE SAINT

'Abd al-Ghani descended from a family of religious scholars that included many eminent lawyers but no Sufis. The Nabulusis were well-respected in Damascus but were not among those that controlled any of the top official posts. 'Abd al-Ghani's great grandfather Isma'il (1530–1585) did hold the post of Chief Jurisconsult of the Shafi'is, and 'Abd al-Ghani himself briefly held that of the Chief Jurisconsult of the Hanafis, but the Nabulusis were remembered more for their scholarly contributions than for their official presence.

Al-Nabulusis prided themselves on their ancestral lineage to two eminent roots: the Jama'a and Qudama families. Through the Qudama family they trace their genealogy back to the Prophet's companion and second Caliph 'Umar b. al-Khattab (d. 644). Both the Qudama and Jama'a families are associated with the city of Jerusalem, and are often referred to as *al-maqadisa*, "the folks from Jerusalem." The family name al-Nabulusi, "the one from Nablus," however, identifies the family with the Palestinian city of Nablus, a historic town of Roman origin located about sixty-three kilometres north of Jerusalem.

The Jama'a family is known to have originated from the Syrian town of Hama, which is located about 200 kilometres north of Damascus. In the twelfth century, an eminent member of the family moved to Damascus for study and toward the end of his life, he moved again to Jerusalem, where he wished to die and be buried. Having gone with him, his family stayed in Jerusalem, where they prospered and rose to fame as incumbents of key positions, such as that of the Preacher at the famous Aqsa Mosque, Chief Judge of the city, and eminent teaching posts (Sirriyeh, 2001). Some two and a half centuries later, another member of the family decided to return to Damascus. On his way, he settled in the town of Nablus for a while, and upon arrival in Damascus shortly after the Ottoman takeover he was identified as al-Nabulusi, "the one from Nablus," a reference that eventually eclipsed the familial relation to the Jama'a tribe.

The Qudama family is known to have migrated to Damascus from Jamma'il, a village near Nablus, fearing the persecution of the Crusaders in the twelfth century. They settled near the Eastern Gate of Damascus before moving to a deserted place at the foothill of Qasiyun. Soon, they became widely known in Damascus and admired for their piety and high standing in religious sciences. Many moved to live nearby and the deserted, nameless hilly area grew in population to become known as al-Salihiyya. According to the Damascene historian Ibn Tulun, the name refers either to the piety of the Qudama family (al-Salihiyya, "the pious folk") or to the mosque of Abi Salih, near the Eastern Gate of Damascus, where they had first stayed (al-Salihiyya, the folks associated with the mosque of Abi Salih). Al-Salihiyya was the suburb where Sultan Selim had built the tomb of Ibn 'Arabi (*Qala'id*, 1:65).

Three figures of the al-Nabulusi family were mainly responsible for its fame and prosperity in Damascus: 'Abd al-Ghani's great grandfather Isma'il, also known as Abi al-Fida' 'Imad al-Din (1530–1585), his father Isma'il (1617–1652), and 'Abd al-Ghani himself (1641–1731).

'Abd al-Ghani's Great Grandfather

'Abd al-Ghani's great grandfather Isma'il was a distinguished scholar, a charismatic teacher, and a leader with considerable wealth and political clout. He was celebrated as "shaykh al-Islam by merit and the knower of his epoch by agreement," and "the teacher of the age and the unicum of the time" (*Haqiqa*, 1:58; *Kawakib*, 3:117). He studied logic, linguistics, prophetic tradition, Qur'anic interpretation, theology, and Islamic law with the leading authorities of his time and excelled in literature and religious sciences. He taught at the prominent schools of Damascus: the house of *hadith* in al-Ashrafiyya, the Schools of Shamiyya, Darwishiyya, and 'Adiliyya, as well as the Umayyad mosque. He was well respected among the governors and the judges, and his intercessions were always accepted (*Haqiqa*, 1:62). He was a close friend of Darwish Basha (d. 1579), one of the few Ottoman governors to be well loved by the Damascenes, who was appointed in 1571. When Darwish Basha built his grand mosque, al-Darwishiyya, and appointed two principal teachers to teach the Shafi'i and Hanafi laws, he chose Isma'il for the Shafi'i post and set up an endowment to keep it in al-Nabulusi's family. He also gave him the teaching post in the great 'Adiliyya School (*Kawakib*, 3:135).

Isma'il was known for his eloquent, engaging, and inspiring presentations, which were described by his colleagues as "the gentle breeze when it blows, and the flourishing garden when the fragrance of the blossom flows" (*Haqiqa*, 1:62). His classes were said to have been always crowded. After the death of the leading Damascene jurist and *hadith* scholar Badr al-Din al-Ghazzi (1499–1577), Isma'il became the top religious authority in Damascus.

Isma'il accumulated considerable wealth from his official posts as well as from his investment in rental farms. He rented villages and farms and made profits from selling agricultural crops. This enabled him to collect a massive library, the size of which was rarely matched. Although he was a sensitive poet, he was not known as a man of spirituality and ascetic inclinations, but one with material wealth and authority, with servants and properties, with connections and immense political influence. He corresponded with the top religious authorities in Istanbul and his favours were sought by top Damascene jurists and officials. He was trilingual, fluent in Arabic, Persian, and Ottoman Turkish, an Ash'ari in his belief (following the famous orthodox theologian Abu al-Hasan al-Ash'ari, d. 935–936) and a Shafi'i in his law school. He remained the Chief Shafi'i Mufti and Head of Shafi'i notables until his death. He wrote several commentaries on key religious texts, but was particularly known as the "author of the tract" for a piece he wrote upon a request from some governors in refutation of the Druze doctrine (*Haqiqa*, 1:63). His funeral was said to have attracted a huge crowd and he was buried in a grave endowed by Darwish Basha, in the northern part of Bab al-Saghir cemetery in Damascus. Isma'il bought the family house in the Perfume Sellers' market ('Anbariyyin), directly behind the Umayyad mosque, opposite the southern gate.

'Abd al-Ghani's Father

After the rise of the family's fortune and the ascendency of its name, there was a brief hiatus with Isma'il's son 'Abd al-Ghani (d. 1622), known as Zayn al-Din, who was described as an intelligent student that tried hard to live up to the high expectations his family had of him but who remained a modest scholar. He possessed a gentle and witty character and was generous to the extent of squandering much of the wealth he had inherited from his parents. He was the legitimate successor to his father's teaching position at al-Darwishiyya, but he was at first too young and later too incompetent to fulfil the duties of the post, so it was assumed temporarily by his teacher. He is known for a modest commentary on al-Suyuti's famous *hadith* book on prophetic traditions, *The Small Compendium*.

The family reputation was restored with 'Abd al-Ghani's father Isma'il al-Nabulusi, who despite his rather short life was able to become one of best jurists and religious scholars of his time. Isma'il junior might have had the intellectual capacity, literary skills, and poetic sensibility to reinstate the family status, however, he was unable to regain the political clout and authoritative presence of his grandfather. In fact, none of his descendents, including 'Abd al-Ghani, were able to do so. Isma'il pursued his religious studies with the leading scholars in Damascus and Cairo. Although familiar with Sufi poetry, he had no mystical tendencies. Like his ancestors he preferred the path of the law, in which he excelled and began teaching in the Umayyad mosque at the age of twenty-two (*Haqiqa*, 1:49–57; *Khulasat*, 1:408–410; *Wird*, 21–24).

Isma'il grew up as a Shafi'i scholar and wrote a commentary on Shafi'i law. Later on, however, he switched to the Hanafi school, then a common trend to align with the Ottomans. The main reason given for his switching was a debate he had once with a Hanafi student over a law issue, during which he was challenged by the student and accused of not knowing well what he was debating. Upset by the incident, Isma'il decided to acquire the Hanafi law from its leading masters. He travelled to Egypt in 1641, the year 'Abd al-Ghani was born, to do so and succeeded in earning a license to give legal opinions (*fatwa*) in, and to teach, the Hanafi law. He excelled in it and later became a Hanafi, a move that resulted in losing the family teaching post of Shafi'i law at al-Darwishiyya. The benefits of aligning with the Ottomans must have outweighed the loss of his key teaching post. Soon after, Isma'il was appointed as a supervisor on the Syrian pilgrimage caravan and was generously supported by the Prince of the Syrian convoy.

To establish credibility as a Hanafi scholar, Isma'il commenced on writing his largest work, a voluminous commentary on a key law text, but he did not live long enough to complete it. He had drafted most of it but only managed to finalize four volumes, up to the section on marriage. In addition to this major work, Isma'il authored several other original texts and commentaries on Islamic law and theology. He was also an accomplished poet with a refined collection that reveals a pious, sensitive, and generous personality. He had a large library containing over 1000 volumes.

Isma'il was a frequent visitor to the Ottoman capital, where he studied the approach of the Ottoman scholars and befriended Shaykh al-Islam Yahya bin Zakariyya. He was given the teaching posts in the Qaymariyya School and the Selimiyya mosque in Ibn 'Arabi's complex, but was stripped of the latter and had to travel to Istanbul to reclaim it in 1650. As a result of his appeal he was reinstated as the Selimiyya's courtyard teacher. However, the incident made him aware of the envy of his competitors and seemed to have had an impact on him. Upon his return, he secluded himself in his private retreats in both the Darwishiyya mosque and the Kallasa School for study and writing. We have an impressive list of works he authored in a short span of time that, unfortunately, all remained in a draft form. His untimely death in 1652 at the age of forty-five cut short his most productive phase. He was mourned by several eminent Damascene figures as well as his young son 'Abd al-Ghani.

'Abd al-Ghani

The early death of Isma'il was a setback for the Nabulusis as there was no immediate carrier of the flame. Isma'il had four young children, three boys and a girl, and among his close and distant relatives there were no eminent or rising names. During the illness that led to his death Isma'il lamented the disregard he received from his relatives, who did not seem to share his scholarly aspirations. The twelve-year-old 'Abd al-Ghani was the only one with a promising future. Isma'il used to distinguish him among his siblings, saying: "In him I see the signs of virtues clearly showing" (*Wird*, 31). Zaynab, his mother, also had special affection for 'Abd al-Ghani, who remembered her with fondness as a loving and caring mother.

'Abd al-Ghani grew up in the house his great grandfather had bought near the Umayyad mosque. By the age of five he learned the Qur'an by heart as was the norm among gifted children. At a very young age 'Abd al-Ghani was eager to attend his father's lessons as well as the lessons of the renowned *hadith* scholar Najm al-Din al-Ghazzi, the author of the famous biographical dictionary *The Orbiting Planets (Kawakib)*, who used to teach under the Eagle Dome of the Umayyad mosque. He attended al-Ghazzi's classes for several years and, despite his young age, he must have earned al-Ghazzi's respect to be included in the general licence he gave his students to report after him.

At the age of twelve, 'Abd al-Ghani lost not only his father, who was his closest and most trusted teacher, but also his distinguished *hadith* teacher, al-Ghazzi. 'Abd al-Ghani was attached to his father; he admired and cited his works, and remembered him fondly. Since his tender years, 'Abd al-Ghani was inclined to prayer, seclusion, and spirituality and his remarkable devotion to his religious duties was noticed by his father. The next twelve years of 'Abd al-Ghani's youth remains a mystery. We know almost nothing about this crucial, formative period, especially with regard to his mystical training and the development of his spiritual sensibility. All we know is that by the age of twenty, 'Abd al-Ghani had mastered so many core texts of the exoteric sciences of the Arabic language, Islamic law, prophetic tradition, Qur'an incantation, and religious obligatory practices, that he began to show keen interest in the esoteric sciences of Sufism, and that he had already read the works of eminent Sufi masters, such as Ibn al-Farid (d. 1235), Ibn 'Arabi (d. 1240), al-Tilimsani (d. 1291), and al-Jili (d. 1428). It is likely that this non-eventful yet important phase in the making of 'Abd al-Ghani's personality was devoted, along with his formal education, to the extensive reading of Sufi literature. Although his father's large library was all but lost by the time 'Abd al-Ghani took over the management of the family affairs, we know that he himself had amassed a large collection.

CALCULATED PERFORMANCE

Through his father's connections, 'Abd al-Ghani maintained contacts with the dignitaries, religious leaders, poets, and distinguished personalities of Damascus. His name as a potential successor of his father arose and he was often invited to join the regular recreational gatherings held in various private and public gardens. In these gatherings, poetic exchanges, exhibiting wit, literary skills, knowledge, and imagination, were the main form of entertainment. Despite their apparently informal setting, the gatherings tended to stage sophisticated and intellectually demanding performances. Participating in such performances in the presence of leading poets, linguists, and literary figures that often involved instantaneous, rhymed, and metered responses to several participants, could be intimidating for young scholars. And a sloppy performance in front of these highly influential figures could well mean the end of one's career.

In one of those recreational gatherings, 'Abd al-Ghani took part in the poetic exchanges and cited a few lines of a long poem he had carefully composed. This led to citing more and more until he captured the attention of the audience. Members of the group were impressed by its sophistication and novelty and being unfamiliar with it they inquired about its author. When 'Abd al-Ghani said it was his, many were sceptical. They demanded a second recitation of the whole poem. Upon the second hearing most of the audiences praised 'Abd al-Ghani, yet a few remained doubtful. So that all doubts about its authorship would be cleared, he was asked to write a commentary on it. He agreed and asked for two weeks to complete his work, but the grandson of the Head of the Damascene Nobles, 'Abd al-Rahman Efendi, who was present at the gathering, gave him three weeks and invited everyone present to reconvene at his place to hear the commentary. As scheduled, the group gathered at 'Abd al-Rahman's house where 'Abd al-Ghani delivered his commentary that came in two forms: poetic and prosaic. The audience was just as impressed with the commentary as with the original piece and acknowledged 'Abd al-Ghani's poetic talents (*Wird*, 32–33).

'Abd al-Ghani's original poem, *The Evening Breezes in Praising the Chosen Prophet*, was composed of one hundred and fifty lines, each of which was an example of one type of rhetorical expression known in the Arabic science of rhetoric, *'ilm al-badi'*, hence its technical name *al-badi'iyya*. In content, the poem praised the Prophet Muhammad and celebrated his virtues. The commentary, *The Flowers' Fragrances on the Evening Breezes*, included a new poem of the same length explaining the first and giving further examples of the rhetoric expressions. The technical difference between the two was that the first did not include an explicit reference in each line to the type it exemplified, whereas the second did. The commentary also included an extended explanation in prose studded with poetic citations from classical Arabic poetry. Both the commentary and the original poem formed the content of 'Abd al-Ghani's first major work *(Nafahat)*, which he completed shortly after this event, marking his appearance on the literary scenes of Damascus at the age of twenty-five.

SPIRITUAL CALL

Shortly after his impressive performance in Damascus, 'Abd al-Ghani made his first and only journey to Istanbul. We do not know what prompted the visit or what his intentions were. However, it was customary for Damascene scholars to travel there to secure official appointments. By then, he already had five years of teaching experience at the Umayyad mosque under his belt and it was likely that, following in his father's footsteps, he was seeking a major appointment to kick-start his career. As a regular visitor to Istanbul, his father had already established a network of contacts, but for thirteen years since his death the family name had been absent from the Ottoman circles.

'Abd al-Ghani first went to Edirne, the former Ottoman capital, and then to Istanbul, where he met with several of the leading religious figures and military judges, including shaykh al-Islam. He was there for twenty-five days when something triggered a rather hasty return. According to his biographer, al-Ghazzi, he met an anonymous mystic who instructed him to leave and head back south, saying: "you have no good fortune here" (*Wird*, 33). 'Abd al-Ghani, who seemed to have had a lukewarm reception, abruptly ended his visit and returned home. He left no memoirs of this journey, nor did his biographers give details about the visit, making it difficult to picture the events of his encounters with the Turks. The fact that he was never to return may suggest that his heart was not in the powers of the material world; however, upon his return he seemed delighted to have secured an appointment as the judge of the suburban court of Midan. Although the appointment did not last for more than a year, his poetic notation at the time of his appointment reveals a deep sense of satisfaction at having defeated his envious competitors. Playing on the double-meaning of the word Midan, the name of the suburb of his court that also means "arena," "field," and "square," 'Abd al-Ghani wrote:

> I was pleased when I returned home safely,
>> by reaching my goals and home lands.
> So you, my envier, may die with your rage,
>> because in judgment I am the knight of the arena
>> (Midan) (*Wird*, 34).

Contrasting Receptions

Two contrasting receptions during the journey must have affected 'Abd al-Ghani's aspirations and influenced the orientation of the next phase of his career. The first was his ceremonious reception by the leader of the Qadiriyya Sufi order in the Syrian town of Hama, and second was his likely exposure to the anti-Sufi sentiment in Istanbul.

On his way to Istanbul, 'Abd al-Ghani met with skaykh 'Abd al-Razzaq al-Kilani, the leader of the Qadiriyya Sufi order and a descendent of the founder of the order 'Abd al-Qadir al-Jilani or al-Kilani (d. 1166). In this meeting, the twenty-five-year-old 'Abd al-Ghani was treated with such honour and respect that surprised the audience. In the presence of his Sufi circle, the leader of the order had the Qadiriyya crown taken off his own headgear and placed on 'Abd al-Ghani's, and later presented him with a sword reserved for the leaders of the order. This was rarely done with a young novice. Then, 'Abd al-Ghani had not yet written any significant mystical texts, in fact he had hardly written anything at all, had no one Sufi master among his teachers, and had no Sufi personalities in his family. His treatment with such honour and reverence as a great Sufi master must have boosted his mystical aspirations. For a young man who is yet to establish his authority this event must have left a strong impression on him, raising doubts in his mind about the merit of his mundane mission in Istanbul.

By contrast, in Istanbul, 'Abd al-Ghani would have been exposed to the anti-mystical sentiment that a fundamentalist group of mosque preachers led by Qadizade Mehmed (d. 1635) had been cultivating among the Turks for decades. The anti-Sufi movement was still alive at the time of his visit and it is likely that he had experienced first-hand the tension between the Sufis and their violent opponents (Zilfi, 1986). This might have been one of the reasons that made him heed the advice of the mystic and convinced him never to return.

Whatever happened during this trip, the experience seemed to leave an indelible mark on 'Abd al-Ghani, making him acutely aware of the widening gap between the path of the religious law and the path of spirituality. It marked the beginning of his personal struggle with the dichotomy between the demands of worldly matters and the demands of spirituality that was to dominate his thought and writing throughout his life. This was first expressed in a treatise he wrote upon his return from Istanbul on the Islamic doctrines (*'Aqa'id*), in which he distinguished sharply between the sphere of religious law and the sphere of truth. Over the next twenty-five years, he turned away from worldly matters and devoted his life to teaching and his spiritual and intellectual growth. He was never to seek the favours of the Ottomans again.

ON THE SUFI PATH

'Abd al-Ghani is normally introduced as the son of Isma'il al-Nabulusi, the Damascene by birth, the Hanafi by School of law, the Qadiri by spiritual learning, and the Naqshbandi by spiritual order. His association with Islamic spirituality or Sufism is through two popular mystical traditions: the Qadiriyya and the Naqshbandiyya. The former relates to 'Abd al-Qadir al-Jilani (d. 1166), the latter to Baha' al-Din Naqshband (d. 1388). Al-Qadiriyya began with the teachings of its master in Iraq in the eleventh and twelfth centuries and spread slowly into Syria, Turkey, and the rest of the Islamic world. The development of the order suffered a serious setback with the Mughal's sacking of Baghdad in the middle of the thirteenth century, as several members of the Jilani family perished during that tragic event (*EI²*, Kadiriyya). An eminent member of 'Abd al-Ghani's ancestors, Muwaffaq al-Din (d. 1223) from the Qudama family, was said to have travelled to Baghdad to join the Qadiriyya circles in the second half of the twelfth century (*Wird*, 24–25).

The Naqshbandiyya order arose in the fourteenth century among Persian speakers in Central Asia and almost all of its classical texts were written in Persian. Unlike the Qadiriyya, it rapidly gained popularity mainly outside its home region. It spread into India, Turkey, and Syria to become, by the time of 'Abd al-Ghani, one of the most popular mystical orders in the eastern parts of the Islamic world. It appealed particularly to the orthodox Sunnis because of its adherence to the literal interpretations of the Islamic law (*EI²*, Nakshbandiyya).

Sufi orders, generally speaking, like all mystical orders involve rituals and protocols concerning initiation, devotion, spiritual development, recognition of spiritual attainment, and hierarchy. The seeker of spiritual attainment, *murid* in Arabic, is often expected, as many Sufi texts explain, to go through rigorous training and initiation rituals. Even the greatest of all Sufis, and 'Abd al-Ghani's spiritual master, Ibn 'Arabi, went through such phases under the supervision and inspiration of a female master. With 'Abd al-Ghani, however, the situation was different. He first appeared in his encounter with the leader of the Qadiriyya as a fully-fledged Sufi master. Neither himself nor his biographers mention anything about his being a novice seeker of spiritual enlightenment. When he rose to eminence at the age of twenty-five, as we have seen, it was his exceptional rhetorical and poetic skills that were celebrated and not his spiritual insights and mystical attainments. Soon after, his ceremonious initiation into the Qadiriyya introduced him as an already established master. After this rather incidental encounter, 'Abd al-Ghani met shaykh 'Abd al-Razzaq briefly only once during the latter's visit to Damascus while on his way to Mecca for pilgrimage (*Haqiqa*, 1:154).

'Abd al-Ghani's affiliation with the Naqshbandiyya came through a similarly brief and incidental contact. During his visit to Damascus in 1676, the renowned Naqshbandi shaykh Sa'id al-Din al-Balkhi met with 'Abd al-Ghani and was said to have given him *al-khirqa*, a white cap that signifies the attainment of a high state of knowledge on the Sufi path. The meeting took place in the house of a friend. Upon meeting 'Abd al-Ghani, the Naqshbandi Sufi master spontaneously complimented him poetically in Persian. During his stay in Damascus, al-Balkhi selected 'Abd al-Ghani for an exchange of homage according to the rituals of the Naqshbandiyya order, which took place at the Prophet Yahya's shrine, inside the Umayyad mosque. In the homage-paying ceremony, al-Balkhi gave 'Abd al-Ghani his walking stick as well as a classical Persian text on the Naqshbandiyya and asked him to expound it, which he later did in a commentary titled *The Key of Togetherness in Expounding the Naqshbandiyya* (*Ma'iyya*).

Figure 1.3 The shrine of the Prophet Yahya (known to the Christians as John the Baptist) inside the prayer hall of the Umayyad great mosque of Damascus (author).

'Abd al-Ghani's affiliation with, and initiation into, the mystical paths of both the Qadiriyya and the Naqshbandiyya, are based on brief, momentary contacts and some formalities. 'Abd al-Ghani describes another level of contact with the spiritual masters of the Naqshbandiyya order in a dream, during which spiritual exchanges took place between 'Abd al-Ghani and one of the fathers of the order, Shaykh 'Ala' al-Din 'Attar, who is known to have taken the order from its founder, Shaykh Baha' al-Din Naqshband. Yet all of these contacts do not tell us much about the sources of 'Abd al-Ghani's mystical knowledge. They only show that at the age of twenty-five he had reached a high level of spiritual maturity and by the age of thirty-five, his name and reputation had travelled way beyond Damascus. This leaves us with the questions: who were 'Abd al-Ghani's real influential sources of learning? And how did he acquire his spiritual training and mystical knowledge?

Spiritual Growth and Self-Making

On 'Abd al-Ghani's long list of teachers appears, as one expects, the names of many of the contemporary leading Damascene scholars and religious authorities. The name of an eminent Egyptian scholar also appears, although 'Abd al-Ghani never sought knowledge outside Damascus. During his formative years, his father Isma'il was his first and perhaps most influential teacher. Under his guidance, the young 'Abd al-Ghani studied Qur'anic interpretation and Hanafi law before even his teens. At the same period, he was attending the *hadith* classes of the leading scholar Najm al-Din al-Ghazzi (d. 1651). He continued to study the *hadith* science and its terminology with shaykh 'Abd al-Baqi al-Ba'li, known as Ibn Badr (d. 1660), from whom he received both specific and general licenses. He studied with several other leading scholars, among whom he seemed to regard highly Muhammad Efendi (d. 1674), with whom he studied prophetic tradition and Islamic law. Muhammad Efendi was the Head of Damascene Nobles, a post he inherited from his father Hamza, hence his name Ibn Hamza. 'Abd al-Ghani mentioned him in several of his works, and in one of his visionary dreams, he saw himself on the Day of Judgment following Ibn Hamza into a house designated for the Prophet, his blessed family, and the pious Muslims (*Wird*, 154–155).

There were other figures under whom 'Abd al-Ghani studied various aspects of language, literature, and religious science; however, not one eminent Sufi master appears on the list. Al-Balkhi and al-Kilani, who initiated him into the Sufi path, were not included among the eighteen teachers identified by his main biographer al-Ghazzi, nor were they recognized as influential sources of learning. Some of his identified teachers were known for their mystical tendencies, such as al-Kawafi and al-Ba'li, but these were not considered among his teachers in spirituality and mystical sciences. Since his early twenties 'Abd al-Ghani's exchanges with many of his identified teachers seemed to reflect a collegial rather than a teacher–disciple relationship. This is particularly so with the Egyptian Hanafi jurist 'Ali al-Shibramilsi (d. 1676), from whom he received a licence by correspondence.

While he respected many of his living teachers, 'Abd al-Ghani revered more several of the remote Sufi masters, who were more influential with regard to his intellectual and spiritual orientation than his immediate teachers. At a young age, as already mentioned, he avidly read the works of early Sufi masters and in his thirties, he was sufficiently well established on the Sufi path to be able to rigorously defend Ibn 'Arabi and to write illuminating commentaries on key Sufi poems and texts by celebrated authorities, such as Abi Madyan, al-Jili, Arislan, Rumi, and Naqshbandi. Qadiri and Naqshbandi though he might have been by affiliation, 'Abd al-Ghani was to a large extent a self-made Sufi master.

Alone with Books

In his private learning, 'Abd al-Ghani relied primarily on texts. In a treatise on the benefits of seclusion and refraining from social contacts, *Perfecting the Attributes in Remaining at Home (Takmil)*, which he wrote in 1685 during one of his retreats, 'Abd al-Ghani spoke of his preoccupation with the words of the dead authors of earlier periods, who were for him "like the living," and of his refraining from mixing with the living of his time, who were for him "like the dead" (*Takmil*, 47). He also spoke of the immense benefits—"the scale of which cannot be measured"—of being alone with books (*Takmil*, 48). In a major study he completed three years later in 1688, 'Abd al-Ghani reasserted the importance of texts in acquiring knowledge. He wrote:

> I have seen in this time of ours a community from all ethnic groups, the Arabs, the Persians, the Indians, the Turks, and other ethnic groups as well, all of whom reached—by reading the books of truth (i.e., Sufi texts)—the levels of the masters, and acquired from them (i.e., the books) the objects of their hopes. If after that one supports his knowledge with additional practice and devotional struggle one becomes among the perfect men, but if one stops at gaining knowledge one remains among the knowers (*Miftah*, 267).

'Abd al-Ghani's devotion to reading and writing marks a phase of spiritual and intellectual growth that can be identified loosely as extending for about twenty-five years, from the moment he rose to the literary and mystical scenes in Damascus until the age of fifty, when he broke out of his last retreat and embarked on a series of journeys. This phase was a difficult one, during which he faced much abuse and rejection in Damascus that forced him to retreat from public life into seclusion and plunged him into periods of severe depression. Yet, it was a highly productive phase, during which he worked steadily on laying down the foundations of his philosophical and theological approach, which expanded his reputation, increased the number of his followers, and widened the circle of his influence.

'Abd al-Ghani inherited a reasonable amount of material wealth from his parents, which he managed well. This enabled him to lead an independent and comfortable life and to focus on his writing and teaching. He also inherited his father's teaching positions, which enabled him to maintain an influential presence in religious circles. At the Umayyad mosque, he positioned his classes on the southern side, opposite the shrine of the Prophet Yahya, who is known to the Christians as St. John the Baptist. He had morning and evening classes, during which he taught a variety of literary and religious sciences. In the morning, he used to focus on the conventional religious curriculum, while in the evening he used to switch to mystical sciences, and particularly to the reading and study of Ibn 'Arabi's works.

During this phase, 'Abd al-Ghani wrote many of his largest, most important, and most interesting works, which included position-defining, defensive texts as well as hermeneutical, creative texts. In this period, his writings tended to reveal two contrasting attitudes: reactionary (defensive and offensive) and creative (hermeneutical and interpretative). In response to the rising fundamentalist and anti-Sufi sentiment, he wrote in defence of Sufism and Sufi practices, such as tomb visitation and use of musical instruments, as well as of controversial Sufi personalities, such as Ibn 'Arabi and al-Shushtari (d. 1269). At the same time, he interpreted some key Sufi poems and texts, in an attempt to sustain the popular interest in Sufi knowledge and wisdom.

Noticeable Absence

During this period, 'Abd al-Ghani met with the renowned Hijazi scholar and Head Preacher of the Medina, 'Abd al-Rahman al-Khiyari (d. 1672), who passed through Damascus on his way to Istanbul in 1669. The meeting was important for two reasons: first, it showed 'Abd al-Ghani's growing fame in the Islamic world; and second, it shed some light onto 'Abd al-Ghani's retreat from social engagements.

According to al-Ghazzi, 'Abd al-Ghani withdrew from public life and entered his retreat at the age of forty. Al-Khiyari's memoirs of his visit to Damascus, however, indicate that 'Abd al-Ghani had already deserted public life thirteen years earlier at the age of twenty-eight. 'Abd al-Ghani did not attend the great reception held in al-Khiyari's honour to welcome him into Damascus, which included most of the city's dignitaries and key religious figures. Al-Khiyari noticed 'Abd al-Ghani's absence. Later, 'Abd al-Ghani came out to meet privately with the visiting *imam*, who referred to 'Abd al-Ghani as one "who saw the mixing with people as a waste of time, and the devotion to God in strict house seclusion and withdrawal from public life as a way for expansion" (*Tuhfat*, 1:124). He also described him as one who values the company of books more than that of people, and noted that many considered 'Abd al-Ghani's coming out to meet him as a special privilege, because "two years often pass," al-Khiyari wrote, "without him coming out of his house and without meeting those who come to see him in the house" (*Tuhfat*, 1:124). After the first meeting, al-Khiyari visited 'Abd al-Ghani again in his house together with two friends, and on both occasions they exchanged brief poetic compliments. In the first exchange, al-Khiyari made a reference to the ill-treatment 'Abd al-Ghani was receiving from his foes that caused him to retreat and isolate himself, and praised his virtuous, gracious, and forgiving character (*Tuhfat*, 1:125–126).

Productive Absence

We can only guess what kind of ill-treatment 'Abd al-Ghani was receiving, but we can be sure that his foes did not leave him alone, even in his retreats. They continued to bad-mouth him, to make up reasons for his seclusion, and to accuse him of failing to observe his religious duties. "Many scholars of his time from the outward jurists of Damascus," wrote his disciple al-Baytamani, "opposed him in his career and sought to stop him from speaking about the science of truth" (*Mashrab*, 24). In the introduction to his biographical account, al-Baytamani gives indirect references to what might have been the main points of criticism against 'Abd al-Ghani:

> I have accompanied him for over fifteen years, during which I have not seen him doing anything prohibited or dispraised, nor anything contrary to the explicit divine law at all, neither in his speeches nor in his deeds. There is no truth in the ill-thinking of him from some suspicious people with immature minds, who distrust the folks of God (*Mashrab*, 6).

On several occasions, 'Abd al-Ghani revealed his bitter relationship with the people of Damascus, describing them as devious, envious, expedient, untrustworthy, and unenlightened hypocrites. In one of his several disparaging poems, he wrote:

> O one intending to enter Damascus,
> > do not enter because in Damascus live the devils.
> And beware for your light not to be put out,
> > by what you will see, O poor one.
> You should run away from people in Damascus,
> > and you should not believe that they are roses and flowers
> > (*Khamrat*, 107).

While socially absent, 'Abd al-Ghani's intellectual presence grew in magnitude. In his solitude, he was more effective. With his prolific output he was becoming more and more popular and could not be ignored by his foes. At the age of forty, 'Abd al-Ghani re-entered his private seclusion that, according to al-Ghazzi, kept him isolated from society for the next seven years. We do not know what triggered this long retreat any more than we do about the previous ones, but this period seemed to have been associated with phases of

depression. He was still living in his family house behind the
Umayyad mosque. Al-Ghazzi describes his mood during this seclusion as follows:

> No one was able to meet with him, may God be pleased with him. A
> tray of food used to be prepared for him but he rarely ate anything, and
> when he did, he only ate very little. I was told by someone I trust that
> every night his family used to bring into his room a tray of food and
> drink, put it in front of him, and leave without any verbal exchange or
> eye contact, shutting the door behind them. And when they return
> after an hour to take back the tray, they find it as it was, nothing was
> eaten. In his seclusion he also rarely slept, and he did not leave except
> for the natural call and ablution and without being noticed if possible.
> In that phase he stopped cutting his hair, trimming the hair on his
> blessed face, and cutting his nails. And when he completed his retreat
> and came out, his stature was deformed from the extreme length of his
> nails and facial hair (*Wird*, 34).

There is no doubt that at some point or points in his life 'Abd al-Ghani
withdrew from public life and entered into private seclusion.
However, al-Khiyari's memoirs cast serious doubts on the accuracy
of al-Ghazzi's definite recollection that it began in 1680 and lasted for
seven years. It is more likely that there was no definite period of
retreat as such, but a series of being in and out of seclusion, according to 'Abd al-Ghani's moods, spiritual states, and intellectual demands.
This is more likely to be so for four reasons. First, the earliest biographical account, written during 'Abd al-Ghani's life, does not mention the seven-year retreat. Second, there are no discernable shifts
during this period in the style or topics of his writings nor with his
productivity that may suggest a break. Third, his biographies suggest
that he was becoming disenchanted, temperamental, and reclusive
even before al-Khiyari's visit, but that he intermittently remained in
contact with people and disciples. In 1675, for instance, his disciple
Muhammad al-Ka'ki enraged him by an inappropriate citation that
resulted in him dismissing his class and abandoning his disciples for
months. And fourth, his own anthology of correspondences shows
that, with varying degrees of intensity, he remained in constant

contact with the outside world throughout this as well as other phases of his life.

Al-Ghazzi tended to paint a more conventional picture of 'Abd al-Ghani's spiritual experiences. He said that in his seven-year spiritual retreat, as do all Sufi masters, 'Abd al-Ghani cut himself completely from the outside world, focused solely on studying and reflecting on the Qur'an, received divine illuminations, and finally came out to outpour the knowledge he received on his fellow Muslims. This, however, did not seem to be the case. True, he did focus on the Qur'an, reflect on its concealed meanings, and write an innovative exposition in verse titled *The Inner Meanings of the Qur'an and the Homes of Affirmation (Bawatin)*. This poetic exposition, unique in form, structure, and content, included 5073 rhymed lines, covering only a very small portion of the sacred text. But this was only one of the many diverse texts he wrote on a wide range of topics. The most important were his major commentary on al-Birgili's *The Muhammadan Way (Hadiqa)*, which took him three years to complete; his commentary on Ibn 'Arabi's most controversial text *The Bezels of Wisdom (Jawahir)*; and his book on dream interpretation (*Ta'tir*). During this retreat, he also wrote on rhetorical, philosophical, and law-related issues, suggesting no dramatic change to his usual multi-faceted intellectual engagements. Furthermore, he was already famous before this period of retreat, as we have seen, and many of his illuminating commentaries on key Sufi texts and poems were written in his mid thirties.

JOURNEYS

At the age of fifty, 'Abd al-Ghani embarked on an expansive travel campaign, during which he discursively journeyed into Lebanon, Syria, Palestine, Egypt, and the Hijaz region. Al-Ghazzi presents 'Abd al-Ghani's travel campaign as signalling the end of his seclusion and spiritual retreats, and his lengthy travel memoirs do indeed reveal a happy, witty, life-loving, and sociable character. By that time, the extremist Qadizadeli movement had lost its vigour and the anti-Sufi sentiment seemed to have subsided. Also, 'Abd al-Ghani's reputation had spread wide and his acrimonious relationship with the fundamentalists in Damascus seemed to have eased. His popularity rose and his books were in such a great demand that one could get them only by special order from copyists (*Wird*, 182).

Sufis are known for their extensive travel, which they consider mandatory for the liberation of one's soul from attachments to material things and for the refinement of the spiritual experience. In fact, not just Sufis appreciated and valued travel but Muslims in general saw in some Qur'anic references a divine injunction to roam in God's lands, discern the beauty of his creatures, and reflect on the wisdom of his creation. 'Abd al-Ghani's travel experiences were not mystically driven or devotional but, to a great extent, recreational and pleasure oriented, despite the itineraries being dominated by visitations to Sufi saints, both dead and alive. The aesthetic and religious aspects of his experience are clearly expressed in his travel memoirs, which represent, in many ways, a unique genre.

Between 1688 and 1700, 'Abd al-Ghani made four journeys, which he documented in four travel memories. He first journeyed to Ba'labak and the Biqa' valley in Lebanon in 1688 and in the following year he travelled to Jerusalem in Palestine. After a break of about four years, in 1693, he began his great journey to Syria, Palestine, Egypt and the Hijaz, during which he visited Mecca and performed his pilgrimage. In 1700, he made his final journey to Tripoli. 'Abd al-Ghani travelled with a small group of close friends and followers, numbering only seven in the great journey, including his brother Yusuf and son Isma'il. Al-Ghazzi described their lack of preparation with amazement and attributed their survival to the blessing of the virtuous master. Speaking of the great journey, he wrote:

> When he left Damascus he did so almost without anything. Together with his disciples and close friends, who were seven only, he energetically travelled from country to country without money or any of the necessities that a traveller needs, except for a coffee jug and the horses they were riding. The master roved with them all over Syria to

visit the places of the Prophets and the Saints that were there, and kept journeying with them from town to town until they reached al-'Arish in Egypt from where he travelled on land to Cairo (*Wird*, 39).

During the major journey 'Abd al-Ghani was deeply saddened by the death of his brother Yusuf, who accompanied him along the way and shared with him the back of a camel ride. His mother had also died only two months before this journey. Her death was said to have coincided with the end of the plague that ravaged the city, as predicted by an obscure mystic, Ali al-Nabki, who walked from his town, al-Nabk, to Damascus, a distance of over 80 kilometres, arriving on the day of her burial to inform 'Abd al-Ghani of his prediction (*Haqiqa*, 1:66–67).

'Abd al-Ghani's travel memoirs of the four journeys present valuable details on the urban and rural environments of the region, on the personalities and social customs, and on the buildings and structures he visited. The memoirs, particularly the one of the great journey, include copious autobiographical notes that his biographers quoted extensively. 'Abd al-Ghani's travel writings are important not only for their textual qualities and representational techniques, but also for the unique literary genre they represent, which is different from the widely known genre of the earlier Muslim travellers, such as Ibn Jubayr and Ibn Battuta, and the genre of the geographer-travellers, such as al-Muqaddasi and al-Hamawi.

'Abd al-Ghani's memoirs infuse the recording of itineraries and daily activities with lengthy poetical, historical, and hermeneutical annotations. The main narratives are not dramatized by perilous events or ominous encounters, but constructed with a poetic and aesthetic sensibility toward the landscape and urban settings. They present a combination of several literary genres interwoven in an original way: travel writing, the virtues of cities and palaces, sacred history, poetic reflections, and religious commentary. In his memoirs, the itinerary and spatial settings tend to reveal more than the immediate reality one experiences. For example, the following excerpt from his memoirs of the Journey to Jerusalem shows his visualisation of a geo-urban correspondence between the regions of Jerusalem and Mecca before his visit to Mecca and the Hijaz. Such visualisation is anchored more in the imaginative geography one finds in the popular texts concerned with the virtues of cities and places known in Arabic as *fada'il* than in actual experiences (Akkach, 2002).

> This is *The Intimate Presence in the Journey to Jerusalem* wherein we have gathered the subtle accounts and fine poems, and what we have related during the days and nights of this blessed journey. It is commonly known that towns have different virtues and distinct characteristics and qualities, both for earlier and later peoples, and that the most noble of the secure towns, after the glorified Mecca and Medina, is Jerusalem, the neighbourhood of which God blessed and upon which He brought down tranquillity. And, surely, it has appeared to us the correspondence between the regions of Jerusalem and the places of the Hijaz. So we have compared the town of Jinin with the towns of al-'Ula particularly as the governor of each is a high-ranking noble. We have compared Nablus with the radiant Medina, for the people of each have in them softness and affection for whoever calls upon them. God-most-high says: "they love whoever immigrates to them" (59:9). We have compared the noble Jerusalem with the protected Mecca, because Jerusalem includes the noble Rock, the former *qibla*, whereas Mecca includes the Ka'ba, the present *qibla*, and because the Quds includes mount Tur that overlooks the sacred places, whereas Mecca includes mount Abu Qabis that overlooks the intimate places. We have also compared the shrine of Moses, peace be upon him, and the surrounding landscape with the valley of Mina, because each is frequented only during the time of the ritual visits. And we have compared the towns of al-Khalil (Hebron), peace be upon him, with mount Arafat, because visiting Jerusalem is incomplete without visiting al-Khalil, just as the pilgrimage is incomplete without going to mount Arafat, whose status is highly revered. Thus our visit to Jerusalem is as it were the minor pilgrimage; for, surely, we have visualized in its places those [corresponding] places in the Hijaz, and we have rejoiced in the hope of fulfilling the major pilgrimage (*Hadra*, 20–21).

In terms of content, the memoirs provide valuable insights into pre-modern travel practices, modes of spatio-visual experience, and the cultural history of the region. They also provide valuable references to many towns, places, and monuments, and in some cases, like Jerusalem's Noble Sanctuary, for example, to the socio-religious practices associated with them. 'Abd al-Ghani's poetic sensibility combines with his Sufi insights to give his narratives both aesthetic and mystical taste, while revealing layers of meaning associated with his spatio-visual experiences in various settings (Akkach, 2005b).

HIS THOUGHT

A View from Without

HEAVENLY INSPIRATIONS, RATIONAL INSIGHTS

On a rainy winter day, 'Abd al-Ghani was walking along with some of his disciples through the narrow, protective streets of Damascus when he was suddenly stopped by a heavy stream of water gushing forth from a spout on one of the roofs. He paused, gazed at the spout, and said: "true, true." Puzzled by his reaction one of the disciples asked: "what truth does a spout tell?" 'Abd al-Ghani replied: "the spout is telling me: 'be like me. I collect the rain water that comes scattered from the sky and pour it out together in one stream, without leaving anything on the roof.' I believe it, and I know that this is an advice to me" (*Wird*, 40). Indeed, 'Abd al-Ghani collected heavenly inspirations and poured them out in a steady stream of works on the people of Damascus. In over ninety years of productive life, he wrote over 280 works in various disciplines of knowledge. His works engaged his contemporaries and played a significant role in shaping the intellectual climate and religious sentiment of the time. Describing the great popularity of his works, al-Ghazzi wrote:

> You would find no one in the world but wanting them and seeking after them. And if you demanded them, you could only get them by finding someone to copy them for you, even though they were being copied

and transferred continuously and much money being spent on that.
And since there were so many of them, they were difficult to carry and
transport (*Wird*, 182).

Although he chose the path of Sufism, 'Abd al-Ghani's sources of
inspiration were not purely mystical. In fact, a significant portion of
his contributions was not in the field of mystical sciences, and his
rational, methodical approach coloured even his mystical writings.
While religion was his main domain of influence, he had several
works that were, in one way or another, related to science, especially
those concerned with astrological predictions and the nature of
causality, which will be discussed later. The way in which heavenly
inspirations are intertwined with rational insights remains one of the
unique characteristics of 'Abd al-Ghani's works. These two contrasting aspects of his thought are best expressed in two substantial
anthologies of the poems he wrote throughout his life: one, *The
Anthology of Truths*, is dedicated to spirituality and mystical knowledge; the other, *The Wine of Babel*, is dedicated to aesthetics and
earthly pleasure. This polarity did not reflect a schizophrenic personality, nor did 'Abd al-Ghani himself feel the need to dwell on it.
Rationality and spirituality seem to have begun to interact in new
ways during his time.

CRITICAL ATTITUDE

'Abd al-Ghani's self-making and reliance on the authority of the
written word had, in many ways, influenced his rational and methodical approach. It made him aware of the epistemological power of the
text and prompted him to exploit his prodigious writing ability to
promote a text-focused approach to acquiring knowledge. In his reference to the importance of texts, cited earlier, he said: "I have witnessed in this time of ours" (*Miftah*, 267). This might be taken as an
indirect reference to the changing role of the text during his time,
especially when we take into account his awareness of the limitation
of the text in the mystical experience and his explanation of the level

of certainty at which the text becomes useless (*Miftah*, 267). In response to those who argue that, since books are incapable of taking one all the way to the highest level of certainty, they are futile and should be abandoned, 'Abd al-Ghani advises:

> I have seen boys on the spiritual path among my brothers who reached by reading these books in a few days what men could not reach by personal devotion (i.e., without books) in forty or fifty years. Yet those men were the cause for the boys to enter into the order, however, as they restricted themselves to practice, the boys became to them as the shaykhs in the knowledge of truth while the shaykhs became to them as the boys. So one of them recited, saying:
>
> > I have adopted my father with certainty,
> >   and there is no doubt that I am the grandfather of every father.
>
> This line is by a man who is a pupil of the pupils of our shaykh, and we do not know for his advancement any cause from the mystical practices other than reading the books of truths until he excelled in his knowledge and surpassed many of the predecessors (*Miftah*, 267–268).

'Abd al-Ghani's numerous commentaries on key religious texts must be seen in this light: they were not merely a rehash of old literature, but rather, creative attempts to recultivate classical literature within a new culture of reading. His commentaries, many of which were extensive, often tended to expand the interpretive horizon of the content way beyond the limits of the original text. And with his style of weaving the original text almost seamlessly into his lucid inter-pretation, he presented cogent and comprehensible commentaries studded with original and valuable insights. For members of the Damascene public who were interested in participating in his public reading sessions and of being socialised into his spheres of thought, his commentaries would have been mandatory reading, for they pro-vide the necessary introduction into his terminology, language, and terrains of thought. This explains the great demands for his works.

'Abd al-Ghani's relationship with the text had sharpened his crit-ical attitude and methodical style of analysis, as his loyalty was directed more toward the merits of what is being written than the identity of the author. He therefore could praise the celebrated *imam* of the Medina Ahmad al-Qushashi (d. 1660) for his insights on some occasions and criticise his lack of insights on others. Al-Qushashi, described as "the *imam* of those speaking of the Unity of Being," was a renowned Naqshbandi mystic, an important commentator on Sufi works, and a transmitter of Ibn 'Arabi's teachings (*Khulasat*, 1:343–346). But this did not render him immune from 'Abd al-Ghani's criticism. He did the same with al-Qushashi's renowned student Ibrahim al-Kurani (d. 1689), who was one of the most celebrated and influential scholars of his time. In his preface to a lengthy treatise sent to al-Kurani, the young 'Abd al-Ghani addressed the revered *imam*, who was twenty-five years his senior, saying: "We have presented our understanding unto you without being apologetic about our criticality, for God-most-high knows that obstinacy and defending the self are not our intention. The intent is to establish the truthful approach on this issue, so that we, and our brothers, may follow the best pathways. God does not shy away from the truth" (*Tahrik*, 46). In another reproachful rebuttal addressed to a Turkish scholar named Mahmud, 'Abd al-Ghani quoted a saying by earlier masters: "One remains free in one's intellectual space until one writes a book or composes a poem" (*Ta'nif*, 15). This shows the significance 'Abd al-Ghani accords to the written word.

From the first few works he wrote, 'Abd al-Ghani exhibited a critical attitude in the handling of his sources. He often conducted thorough literature reviews to explain the literary contexts of his writings, to assess the merits of existing works, and to identify his own contributions. In some cases, he presented critical reviews of large bodies of works with reference to particular themes, revealing remarkable familiarity with a wide range of Islamic sources.

The Treasures of Heritage

'Abd al-Ghani's emphasis on the authority of the text more than the identity of the author draws attention to one of his major works, *The Treasures of Heritage in Pointing to the Locations of the Prophetic Traditions (Dhakha'ir)*, which he completed at the age of fifty-two, about two years after his journey to Jerusalem. It is an index of the prophetic traditions cited in the seven most authentic traditional sources, which is presented according to the first reporter after the Prophet in an alphabetical order. Considering 'Abd al-Ghani's intellectual focus, mystical preoccupations, and thematic interests, the *hadith* index stands out as a peculiar work. It is a large work completed in three months and is published in three volumes.

In the seventeenth and eighteenth centuries, the *hadith* science and its methodology, while forming the core of some religious revivals, were not subject to critical examination or serious rethinking. Quite to the contrary in fact, it grew in significance and prestige to the extent that eminent *hadith* scholars were the most celebrated figures of the period. 'Abd al-Ghani was a competent *hadith* scholar in the traditional sense, however, the *hadith* index he compiled points to a subtle shift in emphasis from form to content.

Since its inception and throughout its development the *hadith* science was concerned primarily with the authenticity of the reported prophetic sayings, the merit of which was established on rigorous examination of the credibility of individual reporters and the consistency of the chain of transmitters. Thus the core of the *hadith* science was concerned with *who said what*, that is, the identity of the speakers, and not with *what is being said*, that is, the merit of the reported statements. Scholars of *hadith* poured their intelligence onto the meticulous examination of the reporters' piety, credibility, personal character, affiliations, as well as the circumstances of hearing, the rigour of transmission, the variations of reporting, and the generic character of reliable and trustworthy reporters. This is as far as reason can go in this science. As for the credibility or validity of the statements themselves measured against the social or natural reality they represent, they remained outside the objective test of reason. If, for one reason or another, a *hadith* does not make sense, the normal reaction has always been to doubt its authenticity and discredit the reporters. In fact the established methodology of *hadith* science and the categories of the *hadith* provide no tools to do otherwise.

'Abd al-Ghani's explanation of the main reason behind writing his index points to some dissatisfaction with the excessive preoccupation with the reporters at the expense of the content, an approach that seemed to have become *boring* to his intended audience. After listing the seven main *hadith* references and noting their extensive coverage, he wrote: "The necessity calls for compiling a reference to the seven previously mentioned books in the manner of an index, in order to know the location of each *hadith* and the place of each transmitted narrative, and for this to be done in a concise way without sloppiness or being boring or excessive" (*Dhakha'ir*, 1:7–8). He then went on to explain that his index was not an original work as there were good precedents, whose approach he had followed. His succinct review of existing references, however, indicates that they were not without shortcomings and that his contribution lies in overcoming their weaknesses.

'Abd al-Ghani's index presents no radical change to the traditional way of understanding and dealing with the science of *hadith*. Yet, his rearrangement of the accessibility of the *hadith* presents a subtle shift of emphasis away from the reporters toward the text and its meaning. This seems consistent with his emphasis on the importance of the text. Distinguishing his approach from the conventional one that emphasizes the chain of reporters and formal variations of the reported saying, 'Abd al-Ghani explains his method and the main characteristics of his index as follows:

> In this book, I have followed the path of those who preceded me
> in its arrangement and have constructed it according to their models
> in its order. However, I have restricted my listing to the clearly
> stated narratives only, disregarding the ones alluded to, and did not
> quote from the chain of reporters except the authors of the core
> texts and in a concise way. I also restricted my listing to the first
> companions [of the Prophet] only, and dropped the listing of middle
> reporters altogether, including the followers [of the companions] and
> the followers of the followers ... I have considered the meaning or part
> of it, not the utterances, in all the reported narratives; so that when a
> narrative of a *hadith* is mentioned an alphabetical symbol alludes to its

corresponding meaning, not the wording. Thus, the seeker needs to consider the meaning of what he is seeking, and this is a common practice among those who deal with and consult such indices. If a *hadith* is reported through a group of companions, I have mentioned their names on one occasion only and in just one chain; this is adequate to clarify the intention. So if you want to use the index to locate a *hadith*, you should think of the meaning of the *hadith* you are after, what it is about. You should not consider the specificity of its wording. Then think of the companion after whom the *hadith* is narrated, for the chain's reference could be after Omar or Anas, for example, while the narration could be after another companion mentioned in that *hadith*. So find the correct reporting companion and then search for it in its place, and you will find it, God willing (*Dhakha'ir*, 1:9).

By placing less emphasis on the reporters, the role of the transmitters, which formed the focus of this highly significant religious science throughout medieval Islam, was made to recede into the background. All intermediate reporters were dropped and textual variations were ignored. Although this might be a technical aspect of using the index, it nonetheless indicates that what mattered for 'Abd al-Ghani was the meaning of the *hadith* more than the reporters and the exact wording.

FAITH AND REASON

During a visit to the coastal city of Sidon, Lebanon, in 1700, 'Abd al-Ghani was presented with a long list of questions almost identical to a list he had received some twenty years earlier from the city of Nablus. The currency of the questions, evident by continued public interest, prompted him to dig up his old incomplete notes and to record his answers to the one hundred and sixty-one questions that revealed some intriguing public preoccupations. One question inquired about the nature of the divine writing by the supernal Pen on the Guarded Tablet, which the Qur'an introduced in several chapters and which medieval literature elaborated. The curious inquisitor wanted to know the mechanics of such writing and the medium involved, whether it was "by inspiration or by a messenger." In his reply, 'Abd al-Ghani explained that it was "by neither": there was no medium, "the writer was God himself." Another question inquired about the language of the writing, whether it was "in Arabic or in Hebrew." 'Abd al-Ghani affirmed, with some qualifications, that the writing was "in Arabic." Yet another further asked about the language that the angels spoke in heaven, whether it was Arabic or Hebrew. 'Abd al-Ghani again affirmed, with some qualifications, that the sole language of communication in heaven was indeed Arabic (*Ajwiba*, 60–65).

These intriguing questions were only a sample of a wider range concerned with supernatural phenomena that 'Abd al-Ghani responded to throughout his life. They reveal a popular desire to make sense of abstract religious ideas and supernatural phenomena in rational terms. An expressive work that reveals the tension between the mythical and rational understanding at the time is a treatise 'Abd al-Ghani wrote after a heated debate he once had with the Governor of Damascus over the mythical details of the biblical story of the tower of Babel that also appears in the Qur'an. Armed with a Turkish treatise on the topic, the Governor was keen to uphold the mythical events and to cite the Prophet and the Qur'an in support of his argument, whereas 'Abd al-Ghani was dismissive, arguing that those mythical events defy rationality (*Burhan*). Similar rational curiosity and debates were also unfolding in Europe, yet in both contexts reason was not trying to do away with the mythical but rather to accommodate it within a new sensibility (Brooke, 1991, ch. 4).

Throughout history, faith and reason have always questioned one another in the pursuit of truth; however, as the new sciences were then presenting fresh insights into the working of the natural world, faith began to seek the support of reason in a new way. A rational sentiment emerged in both the Christian and Muslim worlds, but evolved in different directions and with different pace and intensity. In Christian Europe, faith and reason clashed in a decisive battle that resulted in the triumph of reason, whereas in the Muslim Middle East, faith and reason maintained a dialectic relationship.

The rational trend in the Ottoman Middle East was represented by the works of four groups of thinkers. First, there were the scientists who were keen on keeping up with the scientific developments that were taking place in Europe and on introducing the new findings, especially in the field of geography and astronomy, into the Ottoman world. These included figures such as Köse Ibrahim (d. after 1660), Abu Bakr al-Dimashqi (d. 1691), and 'Uthman 'Abd al-Mannan (d. after 1779). Second, there were the science-oriented scholars and entrepreneurial officials, who wrote on science and religion, attempted to raise the profile of science in the Ottoman society, and worked on cultivating a scientific culture. These included figures such as Hajji Khalifa (also known as Katib Çelebi, d. 1657) and Ibrahim Muteferriqa (d. 1745). Third, there was a wide group of religious scholars with puritanical and revivalist ideas, who were keen on ridding Islam of mystical and superstitious beliefs. These included figures such as Qadizade Mehmed (d. 1635) and his followers, and Muhammad b. 'Abd al-Wahhab (d. 1792) and his followers. And fourth, there was a group of religious scholars who were keen on expanding the rational scope of the Islamic faith, increasing its openness to new ideas, and enhancing its sense of tolerance. These included figures such as 'Abd al-Ghani al-Nabulusi (d. 1731) and Ibrahim Haqqi (d. 1780).

These groups and individuals presented multiple, and even contrasting, approaches to the interaction between faith and reason that cannot be reduced to a single-level rationalism. Khalifa, for instance, was impressed by Qadizade's teaching but he did not appreciate the extremist views his movement had espoused. 'Abd al-Ghani's pro-Sufism clashed with Qadizade's anti-Sufism, although both appreciated the rationality of al-Birgili, Qadizade's teacher. Some resonance among the different approaches can be traced. Khalifa, for example, was not one of 'Abd al-Ghani's sources of influence, yet both emphasized the role of texts in the acquisition of knowledge. They also shared an ecumenical view and a methodical style of exposition that depended less on dogmatic belief and personal conviction in constructing an argument, and more on a comprehensive and carefully measured critique of the state of knowledge in relation to the topic being discussed.

The Science of Stars

Nowhere were faith and reason more in contention during this period than they were over the merit of the radical developments in astronomy. At the turn of the seventeenth century, there were three different cosmic systems competing for acceptance: one was according to Claudius Ptolemy (c. 85–165), another according to Nicolaus Copernicus (1473–1543), and yet another according to Tycho Brahe (1546–1601). The Greek astronomer Ptolemy had almost everyone convinced for 1400 years that the earth was the centre of the universe, until the Polish astronomer Copernicus, in a radical proposition, placed the sun instead of the earth at the centre of the universe. The Danish astronomer Brahe, unsure about the geocentric and heliocentric systems, proposed a compromise: he kept the earth as the centre of the sun and moon's orbits only and had all other planets orbit around the sun. These competing views were unsettling; people were confused about their position and significance in the universe. Although the Ptolemaic system was still dominant, interest in the Copernican system was rising in Europe.

In this period, the works of the leading astronomer and mathematician Taqii al-Din (1520/25–1585), a contemporary of 'Abd al-Ghani's great grandfather Isma'il, indicate an advanced state of science in the Middle East and strong contact with Europe. The sophisticated observatory Taqii al-Din had constructed in Istanbul was equipped with state-of-the-art observational instruments that were remarkably similar to those of the Royal Danish Astronomical Observatory built for his contemporary Tycho Brahe. Taqii al-Din's scientific interests went beyond astronomy and mathematics to geometry, optics, mechanics, and clock design. According to recent findings, in a book he wrote in 1551, Taqii al-Din described the workings of a basic steam engine several decades earlier than the discovery of steam power in Europe (Sayili, 1960, 289–305; Ihsanoğlu, 2004, II).

Taqii al-Din's birth place and education are uncertain. He is referred to as al-Shami and al-Dimashqi, the "one from Syria" and "Damascus," as well as al-Misri, the "one from Egypt." It seems that he spent his youth in Syria and Egypt, where he received his religious and scientific education. He served as a judge in Nablus, Palestine, before heading to Istanbul where he assumed the post of Chief Astronomer in 1571. With the support of Sultan Murat III (reigned 1574–1595), he adapted a lofty castle, perched high on a hill offering an unobstructed view of the night sky, for use as an observatory. In 1580, shortly after its completion, however, Sultan Murat III ordered the destruction of Taqii al-Din's observatory. It was never to be resurrected again. Taqii al-Din survived the destruction and documented the harvest of his observations during its short life (*Kashf*, 1: 394–398; III: 587). He continued his scientific works, although the short five years he lived afterward were not long enough to rekindle the flame, and his memories in the texts of the following generations remained rather vague and ambivalent. This event served a devastating blow to the development of science in the region.

The Pit of Misfortune

In 1577, both Taqii al-Din and Brahe recorded the observation of the famous Halley comet. Upon sighting this stellar event, it is said, Taqii al-Din made a favourable prediction that the Ottomans would win the war they were contemplating against the Shi'i Safavids. In the beginning of their campaign in the Caucasus, the Ottomans indeed succeeded. However, successful Safavid counterattacks resulted in the reversal of their fortune and the massacre of thousands of Sunni Muslims. The terrible news reached Istanbul and top officials searched for someone to blame for the embarrassing setback, especially since Sultan Murat was reluctant to launch the campaign, fearing a strategic move by the Europeans to take advantage of the Ottomans' preoccupation in the east. Taqii al-Din's prediction was considered to be the main reason behind the bad decision to go to war, and, consequently, Sultan Murat was said to have ordered the demolition of the freshly completed observatory. Taqii al-Din was said to have been granted an audience by the Sultan to inform him of the misfortunes that had befallen the Ottomans as a result of his wrong prediction and to seek his permission for the demolition of his observatory. Thus before his very eyes, orders were given to level the building. "One report has it," Sayili wrote, "that the astronomers who were busy with their work were taken by surprise and that the wrecking squad took these credulous people out of their 'pit of misfortune'" (Sayili, 1960, 292).

The reason cited for the destruction of the newly completed observatory raises questions about whether the wrong prediction was indeed the real issue. In his report to seek Sultan Murat's approval, Taqii al-Din argued for the necessity of updating the out-of-date Uluğ Bey's astronomical tables and the useful applications of astronomy in daily practices. The freshly completed observatory had not yet delivered its promised benefits, and it is questionable whether the Sultan would waste his significant investment for such a professional mistake. Furthermore, the normal course of action for the Ottomans in such situations was to remove or execute the person in charge, as it was obviously the person's incapacity to perform his expected responsibilities that was the issue and not the fault of the institution he represented. Assuming that accurate predictions of future events was among Taqii al-Din's list of responsibilities, or at least among the desired benefits of the observatory, it is the predictor who was at fault and not the instrument of prediction, the observatory. One would also expect that the ruthless Sultan Murat, who ordered the execution of all of his five brothers on the day of his ascension to the throne and organized the assassination of his grand minister Sokullu, who was a strong supporter of Taqii al-Din, not to have the slightest mercy for Taqii al-Din. But the real issue was not the incorrect prediction, although it might have been used as an excuse, but rather the science of stars itself.

Sultan Murat would have been acting upon the advice of the influential *ulama*, who were then growing hostile to this foreign science and highly suspicious of the new ideas that were being channelled through it from the Christian infidels. In fact, according to Sayili, it was the Chief Jurisconsult Shams al-Din Qadizade (d. 1580) who convinced Sultan Murat to destroy the observatory (Sayili, 1960, 292). This event shows that it was the legitimacy of the science of stars that was the main point of contention and that the battle for the merit of astronomy was being fought on the religious front, wherein the scientists had no say. The destruction of the observatory was the result of a long struggle between scientists and religious authorities over the merit of this precarious branch of knowledge that seemed to give power to "pry into the secrets of nature" (Sayili, 1960, 292). Although key scholars of the period, such as Tashkubrizade (1495–1561) and later Hajji Khalifa, had distinguished clearly between astrology and astronomy, "many of the *ulama*," Khalifa reports, "were pushing for the prohibition of the science of stars altogether" (*Kashf*, 1:178). In the introduction to his renowned dictionary of science, *The Key of Happiness and the Lamp of Sovereignty in the Subjects of Sciences ('Ulum)*, even Tashkubrizade himself was vehemently opposed to natural philosophy, and especially the school of the famous Persian mathematician, astronomer, and philosopher Nasir al-Din al-Tusi (d. 1274). "Beware, beware of them," he wrote, "for working with their wisdom is prohibited in our law. They are far more harmful to the Muslim public than the Jews and the Christians, because they conceal themselves in the garb of the people of Islam" (*'Ulum*, 1:31). Taqii al-Din's experience can be seen as signalling the triumph of religious authority and the retreat of the scientific enterprise in the region.

The Concealed Pearls

About ninety years after the destruction of Taqii al-Din's observatory, 'Abd al-Ghani, then forty, wrote *The Concealed Pearls in the Legality of Predicting Future Events (Lu'lu')*, indicating that the debate over this issue had lingered on. He did not refer to Taqii al-Din's case specifically but examined the issue of prediction theoretically with reference to religion and the law. He was on the verge of his main period of depression and hence the issue must have been of such significance to warrant his attention. His preface indicates that he was approached, probably from abroad, to provide insights into this controversial matter:

> This is a letter I wrote as a reply and sent as a correspondence, revealing in it the legality of what has been going on among the people about the prediction of future events. I have dispelled the confusion, explained the ways in which the mind and the senses may have access to the unknown cosmic events, and distinguished between what is acceptable and not acceptable in such matters (*Lu'lu'*, 79).

'Abd al-Ghani's treatment of this sensitive issue, which straddles science and religion, reveals a mode of thinking that tries to confer a sense of legitimacy on both realms; one that is neither purely rational nor purely mystical but somewhere in between. His argument reveals an understanding of the interdependency between science and religion, showing the role of faith and reason on this issue within a hierarchical perspective. He begins by pointing out that according to the Qur'an (27:25), God has some concealed things in the heavens and in the earth, and prophecies are simply attempts to uncover some of these concealed things. There are heavenly and earthly causes responsible for regulating the world, he adds, and "those who understand the heavenly and earthly causes can know what God had concealed in them" (*Lu'lu'*, 80). Accordingly, he distinguished among four types of sciences upon which prophecies are based: divine revelation, mystical disclosure, astronomy, and astrology. The first two are restricted to prophets and saints, while the other two are available to everyone else, including scientists be they believers or unbelievers. This polarity distinguishes between spiritual sciences that are based on heavenly causes and rational sciences that are based on earthly causes. Those of the "earthly causes," he explains, use reason to rise from the rational to the supra-rational, whereas those of "heavenly causes" descend from the supra-rational to the rational. The former is merely guesswork aided by various signs and references without certainty, whereas the latter is revelatory and with certainty (*Lu'lu'*, 82–92).

'Abd al-Ghani's rationalization of the nature of prophecies is in a sense an attempt to defend the Sufis, who are known for their mystical predictions, from the attacks of the rationalist *ulama*. He uses rational argumentation to legitimize the supra-rational. In this as in many other works, he argued his position from two perspectives: according to tradition and according to reason. This dialectical relationship between the rational and the supra-rational characterized not only 'Abd al-Ghani's approach but also the rationalism of the period in general and distinguished it from the noticeably fervent rational trends that began to dominate European thinking at the time.

ENLIGHTENMENT AND THE PRIMACY OF REASON

In the European experience, the seventeenth and eighteenth centuries mark an exciting period of change that is commonly characterized as the age of curiosity, scientific revolution, and the Enlightenment. It is the period most important for the emergence of modernity and the making of the modern world as we know it. In 1784, the German journal *Berlin Monthly* announced a competition to answer the question "What is Enlightenment?" Immanuel Kant (1724–1804), one of the most celebrated philosophers of the Enlightenment, contributed an essay in which he wrote:

> Enlightenment is man's release from his self-incurred tutelage.
> Tutelage is man's inability to make use of his understanding without direction from another. Self-incurred is this tutelage when its cause lies not in lack of reason but in lack of resolution and courage to use it without direction from another. *Sapere aude!* [Dare to know!] "Have courage to use your own reason!"—that is the motto of enlightenment (Hyland *et al*, 2003, 54).

The belief in the autonomy and credibility of human reason and the emphasis on its use unaided by external sources and uninhibited by authority and tradition formed the core of the Enlightenment. This is the point where most definitions of the phenomenon intersect; however, there are ongoing debates about almost everything else to do with the Enlightenment. Some view the Enlightenment as totalitarian a system as the tradition it sought to discredit, with its own forms of domination that were constructed "to secure itself against the return of the mythic" (Horkheimer and Adorno, 1973). Others see it as being inspired by "shallow and pretentious intellectualism, unreasonable contempt for tradition and authority" (*Oxford English Dictionary*, 2nd ed., Dupré, 2004, 1). The when, where, who, and what of the Enlightenment, and how truly enlightening the Enlightenment was, might all still be the subject of scholarly debates, but there is little disagreement about the significance of the seventeenth- and eighteenth-century events in shaping up the modern world and its regimes of rationality. Modes of rationality and irrationality as they have come to regulate our thinking and understanding today have their roots in the European Enlightenment; they constitute the heart of modernity and the modern ways of thinking.

Understood as a tendency rather than a movement, the Enlightenment's emphasis on the autonomous use of reason meant specifically its critical applications: it was essentially a tendency toward critical inquiry (Black, 1999). In this new intellectual context, the perennial conflict between faith and reason resurfaced with a renewed drive to rethink the relationship between God, man, and the world from an unprecedented rational and critical perspective. This time, however, authority tipped toward humanity that was celebrated not as an earthly image of divinity, but as an embodiment of a unique rationality that empowers humans to be the masters of their own destiny. Thus, fulfilling human earthly needs and improving human living conditions formed the guiding vision in the search for social justice and individual happiness.

Eighteenth-century France is often seen as the cradle of the Enlightenment with the pioneering works of Voltaire (1694–1778), Montesquieu (1689–1755), Diderot (1713–1784), and d'Alembert (1717–1783), who made significant contributions to literature, philosophy, mathematics, and social science. Diderot and d'Alembert are recognized for conceiving and producing the *Encyclopédie*, the revolutionary compendium that changed the traditional approaches to the classification, presentation, and communication of knowledge. Yet the intellectual scope of the Enlightenment has been widened to encompass the achievements of many figures across Europe, such as, to name a few, Galileo (1564–1642), Kepler (1571–1630) and Newton (1642–1727), who laid the foundations of modern astronomy and physics, closing permanently the chapters of Ptolemy and Aristotle; René Descartes (1596–1650), who provided the philosophical framework for modern science; Hugo Grotius (1583–1645), who initiated international law; Thomas Hobbes (1588–1679) and John Locke (1632–1704), who started modern political theories; and Mary Astell (1668–1731), who raised the issue of gender in society and fought for women's rights.

The Enlightenment was a complex phenomenon that introduced radical changes into almost all aspects of individual and social life as well as government and the state. The changes were enabled by, on the one hand, critical rethinking of man and human nature, of God and the natural world, and of religion and dogmatic beliefs, and on the other, by the development of new methods of scientific inquiry and new approaches to the production and communication of knowledge. The Enlightenment thinkers articulated political rights and responsibilities in the state, projected the principles of international law, rethought the role of gender in society, and espoused a humanistic vision for moral principles, punishment, and social justice. In doing so, they laid the foundation for the modern civil society.

The Enlightenment reveals several characteristics at the individual, social, and state levels, all of which can, in one form or another, be related to the changing attitude toward religion and religious authority. These characteristics are:

1. The tension between faith and reason, religion and science; the emphasis on human reason and the rise of secularism; the rationalization of religious knowledge; and the rise of anti-religious sentiment.

2. The preoccupation with nature and the natural and the emergence of mechanical philosophy and natural theology.
3. The rise of anthropology and associated paradigm shift in dealing with otherness: from faith and unbelief to knowledge and ignorance.
4. The emergence of the public sphere and associated spaces of extended sociality, such as the salons, the coffee houses, and the Masonic lodges; the wide spread of print culture; and the shift from individual to institutional authority.

The intellectual achievements of the Enlightenment loomed against a paradoxical background. In the seventeenth century, bloody wars were continually waged in Europe yet remarkable scientific discoveries were made. Awareness of humanistic values and social and political freedom grew, yet Europeans raced to colonize, exploit, and dehumanize others. The strong European states fought one another while at the same time they entered into worldwide competition for wealth and power. Warfare grew increasingly complex and expensive, forcing European governments to invest in research to develop military technology. The seventeenth century was consequently an age of revolution not only in science and technology but also in military advancement. This provided an edge in wars against other powers, which enabled the Europeans to defeat other nations relatively easily. The empowered European began to colonize the world, starting with America and Asia. The Dutch, French, Spanish, Portuguese, English, and others, all struggled to extend and maintain their colonies and trading posts in the distant corners of the globe, with profound and permanent consequences for the whole world. The Ottomans retreated against the rising power of Europe, and by the end of the eighteenth century, their once prosperous and powerful empire became known as the "sick man of Europe." An interest in the Muslim world, as an exciting object of anthropological exploration, emerged and the publication of the first English translation of the Qur'an appeared in 1734.

Science versus Religion

In 1745, the bell tower of St. Mark's Cathedral in Venice was badly damaged by lightning. It was neither the first time nor the only tower to be struck by the awesome power of nature. Reluctant to interfere with divine providence as enacted through the forces of nature, the clergy had no other choice but to keep repairing the tower. Around the same time, scientists, such as Benjamin Franklin (1706–1790), were working on deciphering the electrical nature of lightning and within a few years the technology of conducting rods became readily available. But the clergy remained uninterested in the scientific solution. St. Mark's tower was struck again in 1761 and again in 1762. It was not until 1766 that the clergy finally gave in to the scientific argument and allowed the installation of a lightning rod, saving the tower from further rounds of natural destruction (Brooke, 1991, 2).

This story is often told to show, on the one hand, the distinct approaches of science and religion to dealing with the natural phenomena that reached a new level of separation during the Enlightenment, and, on the other, the growing authority of science at the expense of religion. Throughout history, science has been closely tied with religion, and up to the sixteenth century, one would find it difficult to clearly delineate the borders that separated the two domains. The purview of religion had always encompassed a wide range of scientific undertakings, and many medieval scientists were well versed in religion, including the most famous of all, Copernicus. In fact, the words "science" and "scientist" did not take the definitive sense we are familiar with today until the nineteenth century, although the roots of divergence from religion emerged during the Enlightenment. Today, the common perception of science and religion as being not only independent of one another but also in conflict is largely the legacy of the Enlightenment. It was during the Enlightenment when faith and reason began to oppose one another and when the pursuit of science began to take a clearly distinct path from religion, notwithstanding that many leading scientists, like Newton, for example, were deeply religious (Brooke, 1991, ch. 5).

According to a popular narrative in the history of science, the fall-out between science and religion began with Copernicus's discovery of the heliocentric system. This marked a critical turning point in world history, after which the natural world that both science and religion were keen to understand, study, and explain, was no longer the same for scientists and priests. The divergence did not happen overnight, of course; it took some two hundred years and many discoveries for the differences between the two approaches to crystallize. Up until the Enlightenment, religion had always had the upper hand at moments of dispute, but the authority of science began to rise during and after the Enlightenment. The clergy's changing attitude toward fixing the lightning rods was a case in point.

With reference to the Copernican discovery, proponents of science point to the fact that the Church had built its authority on the wrong cosmology, and that it was only natural for this authority to crumble with the collapse of the foundation of its worldview. They also refer to the suffering of scientists at the hand of religious authorities, such as the burning of Michael Servetus (c. 1511–1553) in Protestant Geneva and of Giordano Bruno (1548–1600) by the Roman Inquisition, as well as the famous humiliating trial of Galileo, whose life was spared but was made to renounce his astronomical discoveries.

Servetus, who rejected the prevailing theory of the Greek physician Galen, is known for his scientific work on the mechanics of blood circulation and the vital role he ascribed to the lungs in explaining the nature of the spirit. Wanting to explain in scientific terms the dispensation of God's spirit to mankind, Servetus' idea that the spirit emerges from a mixture of air and blood was out of tune with Christian theology. Bruno, on the other hand, was an advocate of Copernican astronomy and is often portrayed as the archetypal martyr of science. His ideas of the infinite universe and the plurality of worlds were clearly at odds with the single, bounded geocentric universe of the Church.

Despite the provocative and challenging nature of Servetus' and Bruno's ideas, it remains uncertain whether both were prosecuted by religious authorities and brutally executed on account of their unorthodox scientific ideas. Some scholars suggest that they were in fact tried for theological heresy and not scientific sacrilege. Bruno, a renegade monk, was said to have declared "Christ a rogue, all monks asses, and Catholic doctrine asinine." Yet, Bruno remained a religious person, although he viewed the Roman Church as representing a corruption of an earlier, undefiled religion (Brooke, 1991, 39). This shows the complex nature of the relationship between science and religion that cannot be reduced to a simple perception of opposition and conflict.

While it is not clear whether or not Servetus' and Bruno's irreverence toward Christianity was motivated by their scientific vision, this gradually became so for many thinkers of the Enlightenment. Perhaps nothing is more expressive of this irreverent attitude than the following words of Voltaire (1694–1778), the famous French playwright and passionate advocate for social justice and religious tolerance, who was educated in a Jesuit college but was known for his zealous support of Newton's science:

> Can I repeat without vomiting what God commands Ezekiel to do? I must do it. God commands him to eat barley bread cooked with shit. Is it credible that the filthiest scoundrel of our time could imagine such excremental rubbish? Yes, my brethren, the prophet eats his barley bread with his own excrement: he complains that this breakfast disgusts him a little and God, as a conciliatory gesture, permits him to mix his bread with cow dung instead. Here then is a prototype, a prefiguration of the Church of Jesus Christ (Voltaire, 1968; Brooks, 1991, 153).

Voltaire's vulgar cynicism might not be representative of the attitude of other thinkers of the Enlightenment; however, a highly critical attitude toward the Christian faith and the authority of the Church was certainly a recognisable trend. In Protestant England, Edward Gibbon (1737–1794) described early Christians as "a bunch of poor, irrational, intolerant, philistine, anti-social, hypocritical and miserable fanatics, whose unnatural beliefs and practices were both 'painful to the individual and useless to mankind' " (Hyland *et al*, 2003, 59). He even blamed them for the fall of the Roman Empire.

In the same vein, many rejected the notion of Revelation as a baseless fantasy and the clergy as a self-serving, corrupt institution, fostering terror and ignorance, and responsible for many cruelties and sufferings of mankind. "All religion is a castle in the air," wrote Baron d'Holbach in Catholic France, which was not alone in breeding and exporting radical ideas. Inspired by the secular philosophies of Hobbes and Spinoza, a group of Dutch authors published *Treatise of the Three Impostors*, explaining that the teaching of Moses, Jesus, and Muhammad were "the greatest impostures which anyone has been able to hatch, and which you should flee if you love the truth" (Hyland *et al*, 2003, 59). Ignorance, they argued, was the core element the founders of religions were keen to protects so that people maintain faith in their teachings.

An interesting incident shows how the increased reverence for science had enthroned scientific knowledge instead of religious knowledge as the true embodiment of the ultimate truth. In an eighteenth-century print tilted *Truth Sought by Philosophers*, Newton was depicted leading a line of eminent Greek philosophers toward "philosophical truth" symbolized by a naked female figure. An identical French engraving, intended as a frontispiece for a biography of Descartes, identified him as the leading figure instead of Newton. In 1707, the image caused a minor scandal in France when the naked female was interpreted as Queen Christina of Sweden who had been Descartes' pupil (Fara, 2002).

Anti-religious sentiment was only one side effect of the growing credibility of and appetite for science. There were other manifestations, such as the systematic rationalisation of religion, that is, the rethinking of religious tenets in light of the new scientific methods and findings as well as the reactive anti-secular sentiment. In his famous *Treatise Concerning the Principles of Human Knowledge*, Anglo-Irish bishop and philosopher George Berkeley (1685–1753) launched an attack on the scepticism, materialism, and irreligion of the age. Many saw reason as a divine gift, a "natural revelation," capable of understanding divine communications, of demonstrating God's existence, and of validating the biblical truths of Christianity.

After explaining the operation of the gravitational force in mathematical terms, Newton, a devout Christian, ascribed it to an omnipotent God. Leibniz (1646–1716), the German rationalist philosopher and mathematician, criticized Newton for making the action of gravity appear as a perpetual miracle, yet he systematically argued that Christianity was in strict keeping with scientific reasoning.

The interaction between science and religion during the Enlightenment was complex and the exchanges had many facets. The growing irreverence toward religion, or the traditional forms of religion, resulted in the emergence of new philosophical and theological approaches that tried to explain the relationship between God, man, and the world in new ways. This time, it was religion that was struggling to keep up with science in order to maintain its currency.

ISLAM AND THE CONTINUITY OF TRADITION

The picture of seventeenth- and eighteenth-century Islam is far less defined than that of Europe: the characterization of the period is unclear and its intellectual history is patchy. We arrive at the period burdened with many unanswered questions concerning the development of science and religion. The story of Islamic science often stops abruptly in the pre-Copernican period with the observatory of Maragha and the pioneering works of the thirteenth- and fourteenth-century Muslim astronomers, such as al-'Urdi (d. 1266), al-Tusi (d. 1274), al-Shirazi (d. 1311) and Ibn al-Shatir (d. 1373). Historians of science and ideas have drawn attention to the new mathematics developed by these astronomers in their pioneering attempts to address the problems of Ptolemy's geocentric system. This new mathematics, they argued, were later used by Copernicus (1473–1543) to articulate his heliocentric system (Saliba, 1994, 1999). This raises many perplexing questions. If Muslim astronomers were indeed toying with sophisticated planetary models mathematically equivalent to that of Copernicus, what prevented them from exploring radical possibilities like the heliocentric system? What happened in the hundred and fifty years after Ibn al-Shatir who seemed to be the last eminent name to be cited by historians? If Muslims were indeed standing at the door of the greatest intellectual revolution in world history why were they unable to cross the threshold, to make the intellectual leap into the new universe, and to give birth to the modern world? (Huff, 1993)

Copernicus and al-Suyuti

About fifty years before the Polish church administrator Nicolaus Copernicus wrote his famous astronomical treatise *On the Revolutions of the Celestial Orbs* (published in 1543), the Egyptian religious scholar Jalal al-Din al-Suyuti (1445–1505) wrote his equally famous treatise on cosmology according to the prophetic and communal tradition, poetically titled *The Sublime Form in Traditional Cosmology* (Heinen, 1982). It was a compilation of statements by the Prophet and his immediate companions on cosmology and natural phenomena. Both authors were concerned with the cosmos, the reality of the celestial world, and the structure of the universe; however, their texts were historically unrelated and different in their intent and approach. While Copernicus challenged Ptolemaic astronomy and its geocentric model, the cornerstone of Christian cosmology, al-Suyuti reaffirmed the religious tenets of Islamic cosmology and the relevance and currency of the prophetic traditions. Al-Suyuti was no ordinary figure. He was, and still is, *the* most prolific scholar in the history of Islam with over 800 titles to his credit. He is also the author of some of the most widely circulated and read texts in Islamic history. Al-Suyuti's cosmological treatise was remarkably successful as indicated by its proliferation in numerous copies and commentaries throughout the Islamic world (Heinen, 1982).

Al-Suyuti's treatise raises more perplexing questions. What prompted such a non-scientific-minded religious scholar, who openly admitted his inability to understand anything to do with mathematics, to venture into this domain and write this rather defensive text? Was he responding to new emerging challenges? Was he trying to defend the geocentric system against radical propositions?

When did Muslim scientists and religious scholars first encounter the Copernican idea of the heliocentric system? What were their reactions? Had the encounter sparked a conflict between science and religion as it did in Europe? How did Islamic cosmological thinking evolve in the post-Copernican period? Despite the many attempts to explain the relationship between science and religion in pre-modern Islam, we still do not have satisfactory answers to these questions. The post-Copernican period remains a blind spot in the intellectual history of Islam, especially with regard to the impact of the new astronomy on the evolution of cosmological thinking.

The State of Science

In seventeenth- and eighteenth-century Islam, religious sciences and literature were the domains of high culture and social prestige, whereas natural and intellectual sciences, often referred to as foreign sciences, such as astronomy and philosophy, were somewhat marginal and restricted to small circles of study pursued in addition to studying literature and religion. Standard curricula in most schools did not include components of these foreign sciences, yet interest in natural sciences and astronomy continued (Huff, 1993; Makdisi, 1981). Active exchanges and circulation of ideas in various disciplines within the Islamic world were also evident (Robinson 1997; El-Rouayheb, 2006). Astronomy was important for practical daily needs, such as time-keeping, determining payer times, positions of cities, direction of Mecca, and so on.

After the destruction of Taqii al-Din's observatory, interest in astronomy continued. Around 1660, an obscure Ottoman scholar known as Köse Ibrahim wrote a treatise titled *The Mirror of Spheres in the Limit of Perception*, which was based on his translation of a book by the French astronomer Noel Durret (d. c.1650). The treatise included new astronomical tables and a description of the world according to Ptolemy, Copernicus, and Brahe. This is one of the earliest documented pieces of evidence of the Muslims' exposure to the new non-geocentric conceptions of the universe.

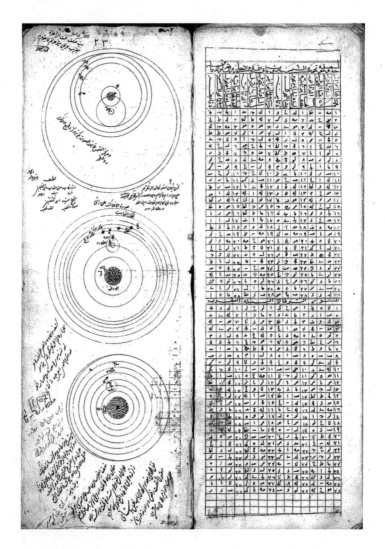

Figure 2.1 The three world systems according to Brahe, Ptolemy, and Copernicus as described by Köse Ibrahim around the middle of the seventeenth century (MS 403, Kandilli Observatory Library, Istanbul).

Köse Ibrahim showed his Arabic translation to the then Chief Ottoman Astronomer, Şekibi Mehmed Çelebi (d. 1667), whose immediate response was: "Europeans have many vanities similar to this one." It was only after the persevering Köse Ibrahim prepared a calendar based on Durret's tables to show that it was consistent with the then popular Uluǧ Bey's astronomical tables, that the chief astronomer was prepared to recognize its merits and to make a copy for himself for further study (Ihsanoǧlu, 2004, II). Shortly after, Köse Ibrahim joined a military campaign and while in Belgrade he further refined his work with the encouragement of the then military judge, Ünsi Effendi (d. 1664), who also obtained a copy. Later on, Köse Ibrahim translated his Arabic draft into Turkish at the request of interested friends and finalized the text. His introduction presented a review of the history of astronomy, which included a reference to the generous support the king of Spain, Alfonso, had given to astronomers and his building of Toledo observatory in 1251 that attracted leading astronomers from all over the world. It also referred to the recent developments in Europe by German scientists, such as Peurbach and Regiomontanus, who corrected Alfonso's tables, to the work of Copernicus, who was described as having "laid a new foundation" for astronomy, to the work of Brahe, and to the commentary on Brahe's work by Logomontanus (Ihsanoǧlu, 2004, II).

Two contemporaries of Köse Ibrahim, Hajji Khalifa (1609–1657) and Evliya Çelebi (1614–1682), were representatives of an emerging new secular scholarship in the Ottoman world. Hajji Khalifa, described as "[p]erhaps the greatest of all Ottoman secular writers, at least in the variety of his interests and depth of his knowledge and research," was a well-respected historian, geographer, and bibliographer. (Shaw, 1976, 285) He was brought up on the move, travelling with his father on several military expeditions. He received his rather irregular education and experiences in this unsettled context, through which he was exposed to a diversity of places, peoples, and cultures. His extensive travel enabled him to, on the one hand, amass an impressive body of bibliographical, geographical, and historical information, and, on the other, to exhibit a genuine ecumenical spirit toward other cultures. Khalifa was considered to be one of the first Ottoman writers to have a significant, positive awareness of Europe, reflected in his appreciation and esteem of the Europeans, and his desire to see the Islamic world incorporating what was best in the knowledge and advances of others (Shaw, 1976, 286).

Khalifa's works exhibit an encyclopaedic character, revealing a rational tendency to collect, classify and represent information in large comprehensive compendia. The most important of his works, *Clarifying the Uncertainties (Kashf al-Zunun)*, is an exhaustive reference on all sciences, writers, and books in the Islamic world up to his time, which lists some 14,500 titles (Arabic, Turkish, and Persian) in an alphabetical order. It is one of the most comprehensive and reliable records of Islamic cultural and scientific achievements. His other works on geography and history reveal the same encyclopaedic tendency, which can also be traced in the works of his contemporary Ibn al-'Imad al-Hanbali's (1622–1678) *The Golden Snippets.*

Khalifa had progressive, liberal views: he appreciated science and scientists, recorded Taqii al-Din's books, and applauded his achievements. His work on geography, *View of the World*, encompassed a broader view of geographical knowledge obtained from Muslim and European sources, including those by G. Mercator and L. Hondius, as well as Ortelius and Cluverius (Shaw, 1976, 286). Khalifa must have been highly regarded and widely read for his works to be among the first to be published in 1729 by the Muteferriqa Press, the first modern press to be established in Turkey in the eighteenth century and the second in the region after the Press that was established in Aleppo, Syria, in 1706. The first series of publications by the Muteferriqa Press appeared between 1729 and 1742 and included seventeen titles, three of which were by Hajji Khalifa (appeared in 1729, 1732, and 1733), and two of which were by the director of the Press, Ibrahim Muteferriqa.

Another important work in the field of science was the translation of the eleven-volume *Atlas Major* by the Dutch geographer Janszoon Blaeu, which was presented to Sultan Mehmed IV in 1668 by Justin Collier, the ambassador of Holland in Istanbul. In charge of the translation was a scientist from Damascus, Abu Bakr b. Bihram al-Dimashqi (d. 1691), who worked on the translation for ten years (1675–1685). Al-Dimashqi was uniquely skilled in languages, mathematics, geography, and astronomy. The introduction to his translation, which he titled *Empowering Islam and the Pleasure in Editing Atlas Major*, reveals the early signs of Muslim defensiveness against the superiority of the Europeans. Al-Dimashqi was keen to dismiss claims by European scholars that the science of astronomy had long died in the Muslim world so that no one recognizes its name anymore. He argued that interest in rational sciences, such as astronomy and geometry, was still vigorously alive among Muslims, and that his teachers of mathematics were unmatched. The difference between the Muslims and the Europeans, he added, was that the Muslims were more preoccupied with the theoretical side of these sciences whereas

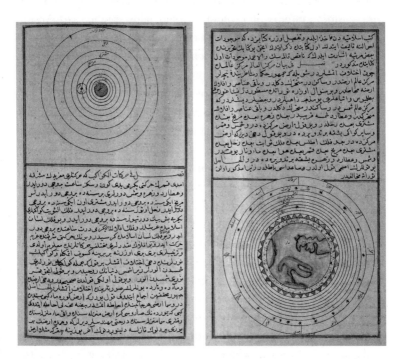

Figure 2.2 Two folios from the introductory volume to the Turkish translation of *Atlas Major*, revealing a preoccupation with the debate over the geocentric and heliocentric systems (MS 325, The Topkapi Palace Library, Istanbul).

the Europeans were mastering their applications. He referred to Hajji Khalifa's work on astronomy, indicating that he "worked on this science a little" but "he could not bring out a complete work." It was for this reason, he added, that the Sultan had asked him to prepare a work on the subject (Ihsanoğlu, 2004, II:12).

Al-Dimashqi's introduction highlighted the close relationship between astronomy and geography, then perceived as two sides of the science of existence, one dealing with heavenly matters, the other with earthly matters. The European infidels, he admitted, had advanced in both sides to the extent that enabled them to dominate other countries in the world and to excel in "disturbing the Muslims." In the chapter on "The Centre of the Universe," he referred to the four cosmic systems of Ptolemy, Copernicus, Brahe, and Argoli, arguing, rather briefly, that the geocentric system of Ptolemy was the correct one while the others, which were contrary to the bible, were wrong (Ihsanoğlu, 2004, II:12).

The new trends in the science of astronomy received more serious attention in the work of Ibrahim Muteferriqa (d. 1745) in the first half of the eighteenth century. Muteferriqa, a Christian convert to Islam, was a statesman, diplomat, and pioneer of reform policy. He was a dynamic and influential figure who made significant contributions to the promotion of secular sciences in the Ottoman circles as well as to the development of the cultural and intellectual life in Istanbul. He was the founder of the first state-financed printing press, the Muteferriqa Press, through which he attempted to popularize scientific writings and to promote print culture. He published Khalifa's popular work on geography, *Cihannüma*, to which he added a lengthy supplement of his own on the new science of astronomy, which was at the time the most extensive text on the topic in Turkish literature. He later translated a Latin work on astronomy by Andreas Cellarius, *Atlas Coelestis*, which he carried out on the order of Sultan Ahmed III. The translation included a commentary on the old and new approaches to astronomy (Ihsanoğlu, 2004, II:15–20).

Muteferriqa was open to the European ideas and placed prime importance upon the use of modern sciences and particularly upon knowledge derived from new geographical explorations. He strove to introduce the new approaches to astronomy, and especially the Galilean-Copernican approach, in an objective way but without undermining the widely held traditional view that had the backing of the religious establishment. He was inclined to believe in the trad- itional view of the world, describing the new views as "unfortunate and useless." Yet, he encouraged his readers to examine the new approaches and critique them on their own scientific merits without reference to religion (Ihsanoğlu, 2004, II:17–18).

In the second half of the eighteenth century, interaction with Europe intensified and selected translations of European works increased. Many figures contributed to the sciences of astronomy and geography, among whom Ibrahim Haqqi (d. 1780) and 'Uthman b. 'Abd al-Mannan (d. after 1779) stand out. Haqqi's large work *Ma'rifetname* gives valuable insights into the intellectual develop- ments in science and religion, showing that the validity of the geo- centric model and the authority of the religious establishment that adhered to it were never seriously challenged. 'Abd al-Mannan trans- lated a book on geography by Bernhard Varenius (d. 1676), and included a comparative study of the geocentric and heliocentric system. Unlike his predecessors, however, 'Abd al-Mannan openly supported the heliocentric system as being more logical than the geocentric system. "If one wanted to roast meat on skewers," he explained rather simplistically, "it is more logical to turn the skew- ered meat on the fire, instead of turning the fire around the meat" (Ihsanoğlu, 2004, II:21).

Religion versus Science

The serious setback that astronomy suffered at the hands of religious authority with the destruction of Taqii al-Din's observatory did not trigger a strong reaction from scientists. Only cautious reminders of the importance of science were raised, as we saw in Köse Ibrahim's reference to Alfonso. Khalifa, who strongly argued for the merit, utility, and necessity of science, remains one of the most prominent

Ottoman advocates of the scientific enterprise in the period. A comparative study of his views against those of his predecessor
Tashkubrizade, who was one of Khalifa's primary sources, shows his
bias toward rational science and his unease with the dogmatism of the
ulama. The *ulama*'s dogmatic, anti-scientific position has a long history, which is best represented in the following statement by the
highly influential medieval theologian al-Ghazali (d. 1111). The
statement was presented in the introduction to his book on the principles of jurisprudence:

> The sciences are of three kinds: purely rational, which the law neither
> encourages nor authorizes, such as mathematics, geometry, astronomy
> and the likes, and which range between being false thought seemingly
> appropriate—and some thought is a sin (49:12)—and being truthful
> sciences but without benefit; we seek refuge in God from sciences
> without benefit ...; and purely traditional, such as those of prophetic
> sayings, of Quranic interpretations, and of sermons ... in which there
> is no space for reason; but the noblest science of all is that wherein
> reason is coupled with tradition and personal opinion is accompanied
> by divine law, and the science of Islamic law *(fiqh)* and its principles are
> of this kind (*Mustasfa*, 1:3).

It is this view of astronomy as "false thought seemingly appropriate,"
or as a science "without benefit," reinforced by al-Suyuti's version of
traditional cosmology, that was likely to have been behind the move
to put an end to the practice of this science. This attitude toward
rational sciences can be seen in the introduction to Tashkubrizade's
important sixteenth-century source on Ottoman sciences referred
to earlier.

Against this authoritarian religious perspective, Muslim scientists
and rationalists had only limited space for manoeuvring. From this
awkward position, Khalifa strove to promote a methodical, secular,
and scientific mode of thinking. His lengthy introduction to his mag-
num opus *Clarifying the Uncertainties Concerning the Names of Books and
Sciences*, in which he adopted and developed the urban sociology
approach of the renowned fourteenth-century Muslim scholar Ibn
Khaldun (1332–1406), Khalifa tried to emphasize the significance of

rational thinking and the utility of natural sciences. He opened his introduction, which he titled *On the States of Sciences*, with a measured consideration of fifteen different definitions of "science," revealing a sophisticated understanding that took into account both religious and secular meanings. This was followed by a brief review of the main ideas concerning the nature of knowing, followed by a detailed exposition of the documented sciences—their subject matter, principles, topics, purposes, and conventional divisions.

In his lucid exposition, Khalifa distinguished between secular and religious sciences, emphasising *human happiness* as the universal purpose of, and the driving force for, the deep desire to understand the realities and conditions of things. He re-introduced the commonly known science of debate as the science of *research etiquettes* or *methods*, and projected an understanding of the universality of science, seen as an activity the very nature and conduct of which "does not change with the change of places and times, nor does it differ with the differences of states and religions, as with the science of astronomy" (*Kashf*, 1:28/206). The emphasis on the universality of the scientific enterprise backed by an independence of the political and religious authorities was a core feature of the European Enlightenment.

Khalifa addressed carefully the religious legal perspective on the legitimacy of science, often presented under the categories: praised and dispraised, permissible and prohibited. He ignored the prohibited category and emphasized that the legal categorization concerns the purpose only. In regard to its very nature as a science, however, every scientific undertaking was legitimate in his view: "it is a praiseworthy virtue that cannot be dismissed or dispraised, because knowing something is better than not knowing it, so be careful not to be among the ignorant folks" (*Kashf*, 1:29). Arguing against "the imagined harm caused by science" and explaining the misunderstandings that can lead to a science being wrongly dispraised, he wrote:

> Know that nothing of science (also knowledge in Arabic), in so far as being an act of knowing, is harmful, and nothing of ignorance, in so far as being a lack of knowledge, is beneficial. Because there is benefit, in

one form or another, in every science, be it concerning worldly or
other-worldly matters or concerning human perfection. It might be
imagined, however, that some sciences are harmful or useless, when
ignoring the conditions that need to be taken into account regarding
sciences and the scientists, for every science is bound by its limit that
cannot go beyond. One of the misunderstandings that lead to misjudge-
ment is to think that a science can deliver what is outside its purview, as
when one thinks that the science of medicine can cure all illnesses,
while this is not possible as some cannot be cured by treatment.
Another misunderstanding is to think of a science as being higher than
its state in honour, as when one thinks of the science of Islamic law (*fiqh*)
as being the noblest of all sciences while this is not so, because the
science of [divine] unity is definitely nobler than it (*Kashf*, 1:52–53).

This is a daring yet carefully presented response to the powerful
jurists who not only maintain the superiority of the science of Islamic
law but also dismiss the usefulness of natural sciences and argue
against their legitimacy. It includes an indirect reference to people's
unreasonable expectations that are not within the purview of the science of astronomy, such as the predictions of future events. By shifting the emphasis away from religious dogmas, the grounds of the
jurists, onto the conceptual discussion of knowledge and ignorance,
the tropes of the Enlightenment, Khalifa was trying to introduce new
intellectual parameters for dealing with science and religion. On the
basis that knowledge is in principle better than ignorance, he could
argue for the utility of all forms of knowledge. He could also argue
that the corruption of knowledge is the result of the corruption of
individuals and not science itself: "how beautiful is Plato's saying that
in a bad soul virtue transforms into vile, as when good nourishment
becomes corrupt in the ill body" (*Kashf*, 1:53–54). This is what happened to the science of stars, he added; it used to be handled by competent scientists and then it declined and became common mostly
among ignorant people promoting their lies. Khalifa also considered
science to be "natural to humans" who could not survive without it.
It is a natural necessity that enables them to acquire their livelihood
and to collaborate with their follow humans (*Kashf*, 1:58–63).

Khalifa's rational sentiment resonated, in a rather paradoxical way, with the concurrent rise of religious fundamentalism and anti-mystical sentiment championed by his contemporary Qadizade Mehmed (d. 1635). Interestingly, Khalifa attended the classes of Qadizade and, despite his secular and scientific inclination, was impressed by the latter's teachings. This is not surprising since both shared a sense of rationality that was keen on ridding Islam of super-stitious beliefs and practices, but one sought it for the sake of reli-gious orthodoxy, the other for the sake of scientific advancement.

GOD IN A MECHANICAL UNIVERSE

Throughout history, both scientists and theologians endeavoured to read the mind of God. They were keen to understand the order of the universe, to unravel the purpose of existence, and to foresee the fate of humanity. The mode and extent of God's activities in the universe is an area where the scientific and the theological perspectives have differed. While both have sought uniformity, consistency, and pre-dictability in the workings of nature, theologians and mystics were keener than scientists on keeping a space for the miraculous, the free exercise of divine power, and the unpredictability of divine providence. Sharing Aristotle's philosophy and physics and Ptolemy's geography and astronomy, medieval Christian and Muslim world-views were close in their understanding of the nature of the divine activities in the universe despite the diversity of ideas both had espoused. In the seventeenth and eighteenth centuries, however, European thinkers broke off on new tangents. As a result, the metaphor of a living organism that for centuries formed the basis of understanding the workings of the universe was replaced with the metaphor of clockwork. The microcosm-macrocosm analogy that was centred on the idea of universal man was replaced with mecha-nistic physics that assimilated natural processes to the precision and self-regulating control of machinery. While all animal and natural operations were reduced to their mechanics, only disembodied reason was granted a privileged status (Brooke, 1991, ch. 4). The implications of this shift were profound.

In the mechanical universe, the notion of "power" underwent a profound transformation. In the Ptolemaic-Aristotelian worldview, the original source of power that made things move, the Immovable Mover, lied beyond the physical world: it was intangible and unmeasurable. In the Galilean-Newtonian worldview, this power became immanent in the world: it became tangible and measurable and eventually coincided with the forces of nature (Dupré, 2004, ch. 2). The mysterious animating spirit that enlivened the world became visible in the mechanics of the clock. The medieval understanding of God's infinite, unmeasurable, and inexplicable power that regulates the world from its largest to its smallest entity began to give way to an understanding of a creator who set all the immutable laws of nature and resigned to His transcendental retreat, disinterested in the triviality of daily events. In this new scheme, man was no longer the original idea in the image of which the universe was fashioned, but the rational master who is uniquely poised to unravel the mysteries of the universe.

In the Enlightenment, the conceptualization of "nature" became a scholarly obsession. Whether in arts or science, politics or aesthetics, religion or philosophy, everyone spoke in the name of nature. Ideas about "nature" and the "natural" permeated most discussions (Hyland et al, 2003, ch. 4). The spectrum of definitions encompassed a wide range of meanings that shared the common view of "nature" as a consistent, self-regulating force of the universe. "A new conception emerged of what was real in the world. Particles of matter in motion defined the new reality. The world of appearances, of colours, odors, tastes was reduced to secondary status—as merely the effect of interaction of particles on the human sensory apparatus" (Brooke, 1991, 118).

Nature's workings and manifestations at the physical, social, and psychic levels became the main preoccupations of scholars and scientists. With this shift, the world began to gradually lose its mysteries, as the enlightened man set out to conquer nature and dispel all

unfounded fears of, and superstitions about her. "Natural philosophy"—the empirical as well as reflective study of nature—became
then roughly equivalent to what we today call "science." Newton's
famous book on planetary orbits and gravitational theory was titled
Mathematical Principles of Natural Philosophy, and many writers even
regarded travel literature as an important source of knowledge for
natural philosophy.

Along with natural philosophy, there appeared "natural theology,"
which represented the attempts to provide proofs and arguments for
the existence of God based on reason and ordinary experience, in
contrast to the traditional "revealed theology" that was anchored in
divine revelations, scripture, and spiritual experiences. Both natural
philosophy and natural theology found support in the "mechanical
philosophy," which was based on the generally agreed view that the
universe was entirely made up of small particles that constantly
moved and changed direction as they restlessly bumped into each
other. The mechanical philosophy dominated most scholarly discussions, presenting a view of the world as a perfectly designed clock,
once set to work it will go on working in a self-regulating, self-
sustaining manner. Likewise, the world was made of particles of
matter that had been created and set in motion by a God who thereafter
made no interventions. The elaborate mechanics of the clock were
analogous to the intricate laws of nature. The mechanical philosophy
excluded the psychic from nature, explained all natural phenomena in
terms of matter and motion, and regarded material things as inert. It
owed much to Descartes' separation of conscious subjects from inert
objects and to Newton's discovery of the laws of motions that reinforced the validity of its propositions. While forming the intangible
core of a universal, self-regulating, and self-sustaining system, nature
was nonetheless seen as quantifiable and measurable by means of
numbers and weights. Observation and experimentation were considered to be the best method to understand its workings. There were
many attempts to explain how God operates in a clockwork universe,
wherein autonomy of nature and uniformity of causality became the
bounds in conformity with which divine activities took place.

Rationalising Causality

In the seventeenth- and eighteenth-century Islamic sphere of thought, there was no place for a mechanical universe. The period reveals a wide preoccupation with, and intense debates of, the theology and philosophy of the Unity of Being that offers no possibility for a self-regulating universe independent of God's direct engagement. We shall return to this shortly. The rationalism that enabled the emergence of the clockwork metaphor, however, was not alien to Islamic thought. Early in the second century of Islam, a group of rationalist scholars concerned with the nature of power at the divine and human levels led one of the most important theological movements in Islam. They were known as the Mu'tazila, "those who separate themselves," or "who stand aside," so named because of the way in which they distanced themselves from conventional theological interpretations. The Mu'tazila tried to provide a rational understanding of the ways in which God engages with the world. The nature of causality and human free will were among the core problematic issues they attempted to address. Some of the perennial theological problems they grappled with were: what is God's role in the cause and effect relationship; when a cause produces an effect, is it nature or God at work; similarly, when humans choose or act, who is at work, their free will and own power or those of God; how can the workings of God, man, and nature be reconciled and understood? The implicit questions were: if God is responsible for all events and occurrences in the world, including human actions, then what is the point of punishment and reward? If human choices are already predestined in God's eternal knowledge and their actions subsumed in his infinite power, then what is the nature of divine justice? (*Milal*, 1:43–85)

To address these issues, the Mu'tazila attempted, in a manner similar to those of the Enlightenment thinkers, to argue for God's transcendence, for the autonomy of the natural world, and for the free will of the individuals. Negating the existence of divine attributes as mediators between God and the world was one core principle of their philosophy; the other was the view that all anthropomorphic descriptions of divinity are symbolic and should be interpreted metaphorically. Their main aims were to keep an infinitely good and just God detached and distanced from the vices, injustices, and ailments of the corporeal world, and to render humans fully responsible and accountable for their choices and actions. Although the Muslim philosophers' argument against God's knowledge of the changing trivialities of daily events was available to them, the Mu'tazila tried to provide rational explanations of how God can at once be distanced yet in control of everything. Their polemics did not convince everyone and their rationalism eventually gave way to another school of thought, the Ash'ariyya (after the founder Abu al-Hasan al-Ash'ari, d. 935/6), that has since prevailed throughout the Islamic world.

The Ash'ariyya confirmed the existence of divine attributes that keep God connected with the world and introduced polemical twists into the interpretations of the nature of causality that made sense to the majority of Muslims. Their main aim was to keep God actively engaged in world affairs, be they good or bad, but in a way that grants both humans and natural causes relative autonomy in the manner they operate. To achieve that, they argued that God intervenes *at* the cause and not *with* it, meaning that God creates an effect *at* the cause's ability to produce such an effect but not *with* it. When a person stands up, for example, God does not create the act of standing by using the person as a passive instrument, but creates the act of standing by making the person able to stand and providing him with the free will to choose when to do so. From this perspective, relative autonomy is given to the world and natural phenomena, since God is seen not to dictate directly what happens and when; however, He ultimately remains in control of all the happenings (*Milal*, 1:92–113).

The Ash'ariyya dominated Islamic thought, although the debate over the nature of God's relationships to both human actions and natural causes continued. Within the sphere of the Ash'ariyya thought, the Ptolemaic-Aristotelian concept of "power" did not undergo a profound transformation as it did in Europe. The Immovable Mover remained entrenched in His metaphysical realm, intangible and unmeasurable yet in charge of every tangible and measurable thing. God, in other words, remained interested in the trivial events of daily life, and nature never entertained the same sense of autonomy and authority as she did in Europe. This ensured that traditional Islamic cosmology and its structure of the world remained unchallenged until the nineteenth century.

Figure 2.3 Representations of the cosmic structure and other worldly spaces in Ibrahim Haqqi's *Ma'rifatname*, showing that medieval Islamic cosmology was still current in the second half of the eighteenth century despite the on-going debate about the merit of the heliocentric system (MS 2263, Süleymaniye Library, Istanbul).

Effects by Divine Permission

In the seventeenth century, the Ash'ariyya views on causality seemed to have been subject to a rethinking by some scholars. It is not clear at this stage how profound and wide this rethinking was since much is yet to be uncovered in this area, but an exchange between two pre-eminent figures of the period, 'Abd al-Ghani and Ibrahim al-Kurani (1615–1690), points to a wider debate. Al-Kurani, a leading scholar and influential mystic based in Medina, has been identified as a key figure in a wide circle of religious renewal and reform. He wrote two treatises on the nature of voluntary human actions to which 'Abd al-Ghani responded with a lengthy critique. From 'Abd al-Ghani's response, al-Kurani seemed to have been concerned that the popular Ash'ariyya polemics did not explain clearly God's role in the phenomenal world and appeared rather uncomfortable with the relative autonomy granted to natural causes. To overcome the ambiguities of the Ash'ariyya, al-Kurani introduced the notion of divine "permission" or "authorization," arguing that the individual's power and natural causes produce their effects by the mediation of God's permission and not autonomously. In other words, when a person stands up, the person does so not just because of the person's own power and free will but also because of the divine permission that allows the person to stand up. The notion of divine "permission" introduces an unpredictable factor into causality and natural processes that deprives them of the relative autonomy they had entertained under the Ash'ariyya theology. Hinging everything on a divine permission that is necessarily inexplicable and unpredictable not only increases God's dominance over the natural world but also undermines the autonomy of natural processes and the predictability inherent in the consistency and uniformity of natural laws. Al-Kurani's concept of "permission" introduced new polemical twists into the already complicated view of the world, further limiting the rational space of scientific thinking.

Al-Kurani was influenced by Ibn 'Arabi's concept of the "Unity of Being," which tends to blur the boundary between God's immanence and transcendence. In certain respects, Unity of Being offers neither space for God to retreat to nor a possibility for the world to be autonomous: God and the world are fused together to form an indissoluble whole. This explains, partly at least, the intellectual basis of al-Kurani's concept of "permission" that aims at maintaining God's active engagement with and ultimate control over the world.

Light and the Night of Possibilities

Although he was a zealous believer in the Unity of Being, 'Abd al-Ghani disagreed with al-Kurani's rethinking of the Ash'ariyya theology and dismissed his views on causality. In 1678, at the age of thirty-eight, he wrote to the revered *imam*, responding to the two treatises he had written on the nature of voluntary human actions. He criticized his theory and exposed its inconsistency with the sources al-Kurani claimed to have used. His main points of contention were, first, al-Kurani's view that the power of an individual causes an effect with a divine permission and not autonomously, and, second, that this view is based on the Qur'an, the prophetic traditions, and the teaching of the Ash'ariyya. In his response, 'Abd al-Ghani appeared to be concerned that al-Kurani not only misinterpreted his sources but also presented his ideas as being universally shared by Sunni Muslims. In his critique, he interrogated al-Kurani's statements, discussed the implications of the concept of the divine "permission" with regard to the relationship between divine and individual power, and presented his own interpretations of the Ash'ariyya.

To illustrate his understanding of the Ash'ariyya, 'Abd al-Ghani cited the verse: "And of his wondrous works are ... the sun and the moon" (41:37), with reference to which he then assimilated the relationship between God's and man's power to that of the sun and the moon. Just as the light of the moon is an effect of the light of the sun, so is man's power in relation to God's. "If one reflects carefully on this," he wrote, "one would realize that one's new power is an effect (*athar*) of his Lord's eternal power. One would also realize how actions occur with God's sole power working at one's power, not with it" (*Tahrik*, 47). Viewing man's power as essentially an effect rather than a cause maintains God as the sole cause of all effects in the world, including man's voluntary actions. An effect can be a cause in itself producing another effect, however, as when the light of the moon dispels the darkness of the night, but the moon's capacity to dispel the darkness is inherently dependent on the power of the Sun even though the latter is invisible at night. This is how God's ultimate power becomes "veiled by its effect, which is the servant's power" (*Tahrik*, 47). He further explains:

> What appears in the night of possibilities is the moon of the servant's power, illuminating with an illumination that conceals the appearance of the illuminating sun of God's power, which is hidden in the night of possibilities. So when we say it is the light of the moon that dispels the darkness of the night, according to what appears to the senses, we actually mean that what dispels the darkness of the night is the light of the sun alone that supports the light of the moon, at the moon's capacity to shine (not with it). The attribution of the dispelling power to the light of the moon is only true in so far as it is being supported by the light of the sun, and in so far that the appearance of this dispelling power is at that support, not with it. And so are the voluntary actions; God creates them at the individual power, not with it (*Tahrik*, 47).

With this rationalization, 'Abd al-Ghani was able to maintain a relative autonomy of the natural processes and to argue for the necessity of the mediation of cause and effect, while at the same time maintaining God's infinite power as being ultimately responsible for all effects in the natural world. Without a degree of autonomy ascribed to the natural world all beings become merely passive instruments in God's hand, and the religious system of obligations, reward, and punishment becomes meaningless. Thus argued, the concept of divine permission becomes redundant; it appears as an unnecessary mediation that only undermines the consistency of nature's habits.

The debate over the autonomy of the natural causes must have been intense enough to prompt 'Abd al-Ghani, who had already deserted public life and entered his seclusion, to write another work on the topic. Two years after responding to al-Kurani, he wrote a treatise which he titled *Returning the Ignorant to the Right in the Possible Attribution of Effects to the Causes (Jahil)*. In this work, he voiced his disagreement with those who considered the belief in the relative autonomy of natural causes as contrary to the Islamic law and, accordingly, accusing anyone holding such belief of infidelity.

In this treatise, he emphasized that the right approach according to Islamic teachings is to maintain at once that, implicitly, God's power is the ultimate cause of all effects and that, explicitly, the natural world entertains relative autonomy that makes it right to attribute effects to natural causes. He cited at length the eminent, fifteenth-century, North African theologian Muhammad al-Sanusi (1435/6–1490) to reinforce his argument. Emphasising the explicit aspect only leads to polytheism and anthropomorphism, he explained, while emphasising the implicit aspect only leads to eso-terism and negation of the law. "Synthesising the two views," he asserted, "that is, accepting the explicit aspect and realising the inner reality, by upholding the lawful, natural, and rational causes explic-itly and maintaining the real cause alone implicitly, is the true reli-gion" (*Jahil*, 9).

Unity of Being

The debate on the nature of causality reveals one aspect of the ways in which the relationship between God and the world was under-stood; another aspect can be seen in the intense debate over the con-cept of the "Unity of Being." The debate over the nature of causality has been based, as we have seen, on a distinction between two modes of being: eternal and temporal. One belongs to God, the other to the world. Reconciling the eternal with the temporal was central to understanding the workings of causality and the functioning of the universe. The concept of the "Unity of Being" (*wahdat al-wujud*), advocated mainly by Sufis, tries to do away with duality by emphasis-ing that there is only one mode of being, and that Being proper is none other than God in his most transcendental state. Everything else depends on this Being who is externalized in many colourful manifestations.

The philosophical reasoning behind this concept is rather simple. If God in his first presence, before the creation of the world, absurd as this premise may be, is necessarily conceived of as *is*, then *being* must either be identical with or other than himself. Otherness implies duality that contradicts the Islamic doctrine of divine unity; therefore, Being and God must be one. This is only the starting point, though, and more complex reasoning is involved when the creation is taken into account. But many jurists and religious scholars disagreed with the Sufi reasoning, some vehemently and violently, arguing that it amounts to pantheism (identifying God with the natural world), and thus the concept of the Unity of Being became one of the most contentious aspects of Islamic mysticism. The concept is commonly attributed to Ibn 'Arabi, hence the controversy he is shrouded with, who indeed might have been responsible for developing it into a coherent worldview, but the idea certainly predates him.

'Abd al-Ghani adopted the concept of the Unity of Being, defended it passionately, and developed it into a systematic philosophy of being. His early hermeneutical and interpretive works, which he wrote in his thirties, such as *The Lordly Opening*, *The Drop of Heaven*, *The Wine of Longing* (his commentary on shaykh Arislan's famous treatise), and *The Understandings of the Unseen* (his commentary on al-Jili's famous poem), all incorporated insights into, and expositions of, the concept of the Unity of Being. At the age of forty-one, he wrote a specific treatise on the concept, *Clarifying the Intent in the Meaning of the Unity of Being*; but his major work on the topic, *The Real Being and Truthful Discourse*, was completed at the age of fifty-four.

The core point of contention in the theology of the Unity of Being is equating God with Being. This is taken by its opponents as a bold expression of pantheism. The Sufis' response hinges on the critical differentiation between Being and beings. 'Abd al-Ghani explains:

> Know that when you hear us say that "Being is God-most-high,"
> you should not assume that we mean by that that "beings are God-
> most-high," regardless whether these beings are sensible or intelligible.
> What we mean by that is that "Being whereby all beings arise is

God-most-high."...There is no doubt that the truthful Being,
transcendent and most high, is manifest and hidden. It is manifest to
every sight and insight and also hidden from every sight and insight. In
respect of its being manifest, all sights and insights see it but can not
know it—"Their knowledge can not encompass Him" (20:110). And
in respect of its being hidden, the minds and thoughts know it but can
not see it. Thus it is manifest in itself, but hidden in its names and
attributes. Because being itself is a truthful reality, absolute in a real
way, that transcends all limits, even the limit of absoluteness. This is
why it can be seen [in its manifest forms] but not known. As for its
names and attributes, they are levels and relations that have no
[supporting] realities other than transcendental Being itself. This is
why it can be known [through various qualifications] but not seen
(*Wujud*, 11).

Throughout the book, 'Abd al-Ghani was at pains to address all types
of criticism levelled against the concept, and in the conclusion he
identified the main opposing groups as: the ignorant boors, the arro-
gant *ulama*, the envious scholars, and the materialist officials. This
shows the level of antagonism toward this concept and explains his
repeated attempts to clarify the misunderstandings and reinforce the
validity of the doctrine. Even though he had completed this definitive
work, which has been described by its editor as "the most important
text in the seventeenth century" (*Wujud*, 1), he continued to write on
the topic. At the age of seventy-eight, he wrote an extended commentary on Fadl Allah al-Hindi's (d. 1620) famous tract, *The Presented
Gift on the Unity of Being*, which he titled *The Firm Statement in
Clarifying the Knowers' Belief in Unity*.

In his expositions, 'Abd al-Ghani adhered to Ibn 'Arabi's articulation of the concept. However, he was more lucid, systematic, and
comprehensible in the explanation of its principles and more
methodical in his argument against its critics. He also gave more con-
crete examples to make his ideas accessible to the public, and was
always keen on citing a wide range of mainstream religious scholars,
especially non-mystics, in order to strengthen his argument and
show its currency and validity. In this, he differed from the classical

masters, who tended to be more reliant on their spiritual authority in presenting their views.

Conversing with the Wise

Not only had the Unity of Being preoccupied 'Abd al-Ghani in his theoretical reflections but also in his mystical experiences. During his last retreat, he wrote *Conversing with the Wise and Engaging the Primordial*, a mystical treatise that records a spiritual experience presented in the form of a dialogue with God. Both biographers of 'Abd al-Ghani, al-Baytamani and al-Ghanzzi, cited this text in full. The treatise explains in a conversational mode the relationship between Being and beings, God and man, on one hand, and Being and the world, God and external existence, on the other. The text opens with the following exchange:

> My Lord said to me: "you are good for me." I said: "how can I be good for you while I am perishable?" He said: "nothing is good for me except the perishable." I said: "how can I be good for you when my character is bad?" He said: "I complement it with my good character." He then said to me: "O my servant, I am you, but you are not me; O my servant, I am who exists, not you; O my servant, all people are the servants of my benefaction, whereas you are the servant of my self." I said: "but how am I the servant of your self?" He said: "you are the servant of Being, not the servant of a being. Being is me, while a being is other than me, because beings are by me and I am by my self. This is the reason why I said to you I am Being." He then said to me: "O my servant, do not fear other than me, because I am that other. I am your Lord, appearing unto you by my subsistence in you. There is no divinity if it be not me, and no one is adored other than me. In any state, if by me that I make you rich, truly, then, I have made you rich; but if I do so by other than me, I then have made you poor; there is no divinity if it be not me." I said to Him: "O Lord, how am I in your regard?" He said: "you are to me amongst those who are drawn near, and so is everyone who loves you: I love you and love everyone that loves you." I said to him: "O Lord, what is the sign of your loving me?" He said: "it is my guiding you to what I love and am pleased with." I said

to him: "O Lord, people are harming me." He said to me: "all of this is
of benefit to you; look within yourself for the result of their harm; you
become nearer to me, and inevitably you will rise above them."Then I
said to him: "O Lord, you are no other than Being." He said to me: "I am
no other than Being and you are no other than non-being." I said to
him: "O Lord, what is non-being?" He said to me: "Non-being is the
negation of Being as the shadow is the negation of the sun[light]." I said
to him: "How can Being be negated?" He said to me: "it can be negated
by the existence of non-being." I said to him: "How can non-being
exist?" He said to me: "Non-being can exist by manifesting Being in it."
I said to him: "How can Being manifest in non-being?" He said to me:
"Being manifests in itself and non-being manifests in itself and then
they unite together." I said to him: "How do they unite together?" He
said to me: "Did you not hear my saying: 'God is the light of heaven
and earth,' and [see] how the lamplight unites with the darkness of the
house, negates it, and manifests in its place and with its form. So
likewise, I negate non-being and manifest in its place by my knowledge
of its form" (*Mashrab*, 13–14).

The theology of the Unity of Being, as established by Ibn 'Arabi and
elaborated by 'Abd al-Ghani, presents a phenomenological understanding of the world, one whose theoretical foundations are
anchored in the experience of daily life. Despite 'Abd al-Ghani's
many attempts to clarify its complex and contentious elements, two
critical questions remained: one concerns the degree of autonomy it
ascribes to created beings, the other concerns the delicate balance
between God's immanence and transcendence.

In the above dialogue, 'Abd al-Ghani explained that in the creative
process of manifestation, non-being, which represents the entire
world in its pre-creation state, had autonomy in itself: "Being manifests in itself and non-being manifests in itself and then they unite
together." He further illustrated this by the example he used to
explain the process of unification: "the lamplight unites with the
darkness of the house, negates it, and manifests in its place and with
its form." This means that beings, while they are dependent in their
existence on Being or God, have qualities and laws inherent in their

very nature, just as the forms and the laws responsible for making the "house" what it is are already inherent in the possibility of the house itself. The light of Being only brings it out and makes it a tangible reality. In the "night of possibilities," to use 'Abd al-Ghani's metaphor, beings already have inherent qualities that the light of Being brings out, makes visible, and puts to work.

This understanding along with those of power and causality espoused by 'Abd al-Ghani was, in many ways, similar to the views natural philosophers advocated in Europe at that time. Newton, for example, saw God as the ultimate source of active power in the world while maintaining the autonomy and consistency of natural laws (Dupré, 2004, 21). His concept of "inertia," for instance, led him to believe that there never could have been any motion in the world generated from within. "Some other principle was necessary for putting bodies into motion." And once they are in motion, "some other principle is necessary for conserving the motion." Although his empirical, scientific method prevented him from considering metaphysical sources, he admitted at the end of his analyses that he was unable to explain the causes of motion and gravity with reference to the phenomena themselves. He spoke of "subtle spirit which pervades and lies hid in all gross bodies," and explained that "by the forces and action of which spirit the particles of bodies attract one another at near distances and cohere, if contiguous" (Dupré, 2004, 21–22). In his final analyses, Newton attributed the ultimate command over the natural world to an incorporeal, living, intelligent, omnipresent Being, who sees, perceives, and comprehends all things intimately and to whose infinite knowledge the whole reality is immediately present.

One crucial difference between the Christian and Islamic cosmological thinking during this period was that Christian philosophy and theology were growing increasingly dependent on the findings of empirical sciences, while their Islamic counterparts were growing indifferent to the mechanics of the new universe. Whereas Ibn 'Arabi's Unity of Being was inextricably anchored in a geocentric universe, 'Abd al-Ghani's version could work just as well with a geocentric or a heliocentric system. The fact that he did not write explicitly on cosmology nor comment on Ibn 'Arabi's five-hundred-year-old cosmology points to the abstract direction he followed. At a time of radical changes, being philosophically and theologically indifferent to the actual structure of the new universe helped the Muslims to preserve the centrality of humanity in the scheme of existence, a position that was irrecoverably lost in the Christian context.

THE HUMAN REALITY

The great appeal of nature and the natural during the Enlightenment inspired a demand for a science of human nature. In *A Treatise of Human Nature*, Hume stressed "that all the sciences have a relation, greater or less, to human nature" (Hyland *et al*, 2003, 3). In contrast to the medieval focus on the universalities of the human reality, the Enlightenment thinkers became preoccupied with the particularities of the soul's conducts and the processes of the mind. Passions, feelings, and emotions became the object of intense and unprecedented types of study and a new sense of the *selfhood* emerged. "Despite the persistence and development of rationalist trends, the Enlightenment could more accurately be described as an age of *self consciousness*" (Dupré, 2004, 53).

Scholars from every discipline of study were engaged in a wholesale rethinking of human nature, exploring new and exciting terrains of social sciences and charting new domains of anthropology, psychology, and sociology. This marked a radical shift from the medieval Christian preoccupation with humanity primarily as a privileged species created in the image of divinity and made to dwell at the centre of a purpose-designed universe. The Christian sacred history of creation predicated on the idea of original sin and the biblical story of the fall began to give way to a new secular history of humanity that was self-centred and almost irrelevant to the interests of divinity and its promise of salvation.

In his *Leviathan*, the atheist English thinker Thomas Hobbes (1588–1679), a graduate from Oxford, argued "that men are naturally and fundamentally self-seeking, individually existing units, who have to learn to co-operate within a society" (Hyland *et al*, 2003, 4). Social existence, in his view, is a necessity that protects the individuals and supports their selfish interests. Likewise, in *Man a Machine*, the French physician and philosopher La Mattrie (1709–1751) dismissed the projective conception of man by preceding philosophers, arguing that the only way to understand the human nature was by empirical, retrospective analysis based on experience and observation. He concluded that humans, in their individual and social existence, are governed completely by physical impulses and that their moral values are subjective and arbitrary. In his famous and widely circulated poem titled *An Essay on Man*, Alexander Pope (1688–1744), England's leading poet of the early Enlightenment, summed up eloquently the prevailing sentiment of the age that witnessed the emergence of a keen interest in unveiling the hidden mysteries of this doubtful yet powerful creature, and of new approaches to understanding the workings of his both sublime and mundane nature. He wrote:

Know then thyself, presume not God to scan;
The proper study of Mankind is Man.
Plac'd on this isthmus of a middle state,
A being darkly wise, and rudely great;
With too much knowledge for the Sceptic side,
With too much weakness for the Stoic pride,
He hangs between; in doubt to act, or to rest,
In doubt to deem himself a God, or Beast;
In doubt his Mind or Body to prefer,
Born but to die, and reas'ning but to err;...
Go, wond'rous creature! mount where Science guides,
Go, measure earth, weigh air, and state the tides,
Instruct the planets in what orbs to run,
Correct old Time, and regulate the Sun
    (Hyland *et al*, 2003, 12–13).

Cartesian Dreams

The most profound change to understanding human nature was initiated by the works of the celebrated French philosopher René
Descartes. A contemporary of 'Abd al-Ghani, Descartes was a
believer who delighted in mathematics and enjoyed meditating alone
in stove-heated rooms. One night at the age of twenty-three, he had
three visionary dreams that were said to have inspired him to initiate
a decisive rethinking of human nature that radically changed the main
orientation of European philosophy. His influential meditations on
the nature of the mind, the body, and the external world are recognized for providing the philosophical framework for modern scientific methodology, which is anchored in his effective separation of the
subjective and objective realms. He defined man a "conscious being"
and saw human engagement with the world as self-conscious minds
(subjects) confronting and coming to terms with autonomous,
extended bodies that exist out there (objects) (Anscombe, 1970, 2nd
and 6th Meditation).

In his rethinking of the human nature, Descartes began by ques-
tioning himself over what he actually meant when he referred to
himself in daily speech as "I." He wanted to understand the relationship between his ego, the "I," and his body. After a series of self-
interrogation he said: "I can validly infer that my essence consists
simply in the fact that I am a conscious being" (Anscombe, 1970,
114). Having equated his ego with his self-conscious mind, he concluded: "so it is certain that I am really distinct from my body, and
could exist without it" (Anscombe, 1970, 115). He then went on to
explain the basis of his conclusion:

> Body is of its nature always divisible; mind is wholly indivisible. When I
> consider the mind—that is, myself, in so far as I am merely a conscious
> being—I can distinguish no part within myself; I understand myself to
> be a single and complete thing. Although the whole mind seems to be
> united to the whole body; yet when a foot or an arm or any other
> part of the body is cut off I am not aware that any substraction has
> been made from the mind. Nor can the faculties of will, feeling,

understanding and so on be called its parts; for it is one and the same
mind that wills, feels, and understands (Anscombe, 1970, 121).

Based on this sharp distinction between the mind and the body,
Descartes was able to separate effectively the realm of subjectivity, of
inner thoughts, emotions, and desires, from the objective reality that
embodied autonomous sets of measurable and quantifiable properties. This separation was critical for the development of the scientific
methodology that flourished during the Enlightenment and was
exemplified in the pioneering work of Newton.

Structures of Light

Perhaps nowhere did the intellectual debates in the Christian and
Islamic world resonate with each other more profoundly during this
period than over the issues of the ego and the body. For centuries,
Muslim philosophers, theologians, and mystics reflected on and
debated this important issue, making one wonder whether the
Cartesian dreams had involved some telepathic exchanges with figures such as al-Suhrawardi (d. 1191), al-Razi (d. 1209), al-Dawani
(d. 1502), and Kemal Pashazade (d. 1534). In his much discussed
text, *Structures of Light* (*Hayakil al-Nur*), al-Suhrawardi wrote: "You
cannot be unaware of yourself, never, but you can be unaware of each
and every part of your body sometimes. So if you were the whole of
these body parts, your consciousness of your self would not persist at
moments of unawareness of your body. So you are beyond this body
and its parts" (*Hayakil*, 49). He further explained that the body is constantly changing by growth and degeneration, "so if you were this
body or a part of it, then your I-ness (i.e., ego, self) would change at
every moment, and the perceived essence of yours would seize. So
you are what you are irrespective of your body ... you are beyond all
these things" (*Hayakil*, 49).

Al-Suhrawardi was a renowned mystic famous for being executed
in Aleppo on the order of the legendary leader Saladin. In the above
work, he used the term *haykal* (plural, *hayakil*), literally, "temple,"

"structure," and "skeleton," to discuss the various components of the human reality. He did so under seven *Structures*. In the first *Structure* he discussed the nature of the body, in the second the nature of the self, in the third the nature of the intellect, in the fourth the nature of essential being, in the fifth the nature of accidental being, in the sixth the nature of the soul, and in the seventh the nature of rationality. Using the notion of "light," he presented the various components as structures infused with different degrees of luminosity and analysed the human nature in terms of transparency and opacity. Seeing both the tangible and intangible components of man as "structures" allowed the notion of the "body" to be understood as a substance with different degrees of opacity corresponding to the level of its density and subtlety. With this conception it was possible to think of the "soul" as a "subtle body" in contrast to the "dense body," for which a specific Arabic term was used, *badan*, that referred to the human body without the head.

By the turn of the seventeenth century, al-Suhrawardi's ideas were thoroughly examined and discussed by many Muslim thinkers. The pre-eminent theologian al-Razi discussed them in several of his works, and especially in his *Oriental Reflections (al-Mabahith al-Mashriqiyya)*; the renowned philosopher of Shiraz, al-Dawani, wrote an extended commentary on the text; shaykh al-Islam in Istanbul, Kemal Pashazade (a prolific scholar with about 200 works), wrote a succinct critique of the main ideas, and many others weighed into the ongoing debate. These major works were in circulation in Damascus and Istanbul in the seventeenth century and the topic was still of interest to the public. 'Abd al-Ghani was approached to write a commentary on Pashazade's *A Treatise on the Human Reality*, which led to his writing of *The Key of Openings in the Niche of the Body, the Glass of the Soul, and the Light of the Spirit (Miftah)*. This substantial work presents a significant contribution to the intellectual exchange on human nature, documenting a sustained debate of the topic spanning over five hundred years.

The debate was centred on the meanings of the term "man" (*insan* in Arabic), the nature of the body, soul, and spirit, and the reality of the self (or ego) and consciousness. The main issues of the debate were, first, whether the term "man" referred to the embodied human form or to something else, and if to something else, what that thing was; second, whether the "soul" differed from the "spirit," both being the intangible component of man, and if they differed, how did each relate to the functioning of the body; and third, how enduring and consistent one's self-consciousness was, and what role self-consciousness played in the making of one's subjectivity and the defining of its relationships with God and the external world.

Self and Body Fusion

In the debate over the relationship between the indivisible, immutable ego and the divisible, mutable body, Muslim scholars advocated different positions. Both al-Suhrawardi and al-Dawani argued that the ego is a reality independent of the body, the position adopted later by Descartes, whereas al-Razi and Pashazade took a different stance, arguing that the distinction between the mind and the body does not necessarily mean that the ego is a reality beyond the body (al-Razi changed position in his works after first adopting al-Suhrawardi's argument). 'Abd al-Ghani, however, took an explictly anti-Cartesian stance and argued against the very foundation of al-Suhrawardi's propositions. His position was close to Pashazade, who, in his view, was "among the best scholars of traditional and rational sciences" (*Miftah*, 226), yet whose approach remains different from that of the mystics. Different as they might have been, Pashazade's and 'Abd al-Ghani's views reveal a break with the position of the previous thinkers, signalling an interesting shift away from the Cartesian approach, which was then gaining ground in Europe.

Pashazade's critique was centred on two related issues. One was the proposition that the "self"—the thing that one refers to when saying "I"—was other than the sensible body. The other was the nature of this other reality that was distinguished from the sensible body on the basis of the immutability of the "I" and the mutability of the body throughout one's life. Although he accepted the basic distinction between the immutable self and the mutable body, he

rejected the argument that this automatically leads to their separation. He consequently rejected that the "I," enduring as it may
be, is an abstract reality beyond the body. In his treatise, he supported
the views that described the self as "bodily parts fused in the
human structure in a manner similar to the fusion of fire in the coal,
the fat in the sesame, and the rosewater in the rose." He further
explained:

> Then the erudite scholars of those (who held the above view) said that
> these bodily parts, which endure from the beginning to the end of
> one's life, are bodies that are different in reality and essence to those
> bodies from which the human structure is composed. Those bodies are
> alive by themselves, conscious of themselves, luminous in themselves.
> When they combine with the human body and become infused in the
> human structure as the fusion of fire in the coal, the body becomes illu-
> minated by the light of that spirit and movable by the spirit's moving
> power ... If you examine what we have told you, you will realize the
> falsity of using the degeneration of the body and its parts as a basis to
> argue that beyond this body and its parts there is an abstract thing,
> which is man in reality, and that it is this reality that everyone refers to
> when saying "I" (*Insan*, 181–182).

Pashazade's reference to "bodily parts" in plural is intriguing. It
raises a question as to whether he was referring to "particles," the
core elements of mechanical philosophy that later swept through
Europe. An interesting comment written on the margin of the
manuscript of Pashazade's treatise identifies his anti-abstraction view
as being that of the public (*Insan*, 181). Whatever he might have
meant, those parts were "conscious by themselves." In al-Dawani's
exposition of al-Suhrawardi's ideas, the ego remained *always* self-
conscious even in the states of sleep and unconsciousness (*Shawakil*
22–23). Pashazade did not challenge this proposition in his critique.

God and Self-Effacement

While 'Abd al-Ghani concurred with Pashazade regarding the indissoluble bond between the body and the self, he disagreed with him on

the nature of self-consciousness. He rejected the taken-for-granted propositions of the immutability of the ego in one's lifetime and the persistence of self-consciousness at all times. In his argument, he drew more on his spiritual experiences rather than his rational insights, explaining that the mystical sources of his ideas were "unfamiliar to the philosophers and others following the dictates of rational thinking," including Pashazade (*Miftah*, 236). 'Abd al-Ghani's ideas on the human reality are expounded mostly in *The Key of Openings*, which he wrote at the age of fifty. Two years later, he also wrote a brief commentary, *A Treatise Concerning Man*. Yet in many of his works he touched in different ways on this seemingly popular theme. In *The Glittering Planet*, a commentary he wrote about six years before *The Key of Openings* on a poem by the pre-eminent twelfth-century theologian al-Ghazali, 'Abd al-Ghani explained his view on the dual meaning of "man:"

> Know that the term "man" has two meanings: one sensible that can be seen by sight and sensed by touch that knows the seen and believes in the unseen, the other is the intelligent self. The first man has concomitants and characteristics that distinguish him from the second, and the same applies to the second, most of whose attributes differ from the first. The first is mortal by nature, while the second is immortal in essence: he is life itself. The first is sensible while the second cannot be perceived except by the intellect. For the established scholars, "man" is the second, while reference to the first as "man" is metaphorical, as when the sunlight is called sun. Just as the light that arises from the sun remains dependent on it and is taken as an expression of it, so is the manifest man the shadow and ghost of the real man. And just as the name of the sun, which refers to the sun itself, is applied to the light that is associated with it, so is the name for the real man called upon the sensible form because it is the medium of expressing its actions and the place of exercising its discretions (*Kawkab*, 133–134).

The duality proposed in this text, although it differentiates between the sensible and intelligible man, does not map onto the Cartesian's duality of the mind and the body. Man remains a unified totality in both his sensible and intelligible forms. This became clearer in *The*

Key of Openings, wherein 'Abd al-Ghani also argued against the immutability of the self. Unlike his predecessors, 'Abd al-Ghani saw the self as changing in its engagements with the external world. He also saw man as capable of being completely unself-conscious. The best example of this is when in the mystical experience man recalls his Lord, and with this recollection he annihilates his ego completely. God and the ego cannot coexist in man's consciousness, he stressed; when one is present the other must necessarily be absent. For 'Abd al-Ghani, the human ego is but a trace or an effect of God's power. By invoking its divine origin the ego annihilates itself by allowing God to take over and become the object of consciousness. "When man considers the door or the box that are made out of wood, for example," he explains, "he overlooks the wood-ness, and when he considers the wood-ness he overlooks the door and the box completely. Considering both at once detracts from considering each alone profoundly" (*Miftah*, 236). This means that the self is not the exclusive owner of consciousness; it is what preoccupies the self in each and every moment that becomes the object of consciousness. Self-consciousness then refers to those brief moments during which consciousness is preoccupied with the self alone. In this understanding, the acts of "remembering," "recollecting," and "invoking" become effective means of changing the preoccupations of the self and ultimately of self-effacement. He explains:

God-most-high said: "Remember your Lord when you have forgotten" (18:24). Some eminent scholars of the Muslim community, who had scrutinized the secrets of the great Qur'an, said: "when you have forgotten yourself." They pointed to the fact that man, in so far as he is a divine spirit, as already mentioned, may forget his self and become unaware of it completely. The reason for this is his remembrance of his Lord in his self, as God-most-high said: "Remember your Lord in yourself" (7:205), meaning that his self is the appearance of his Lord unto him, because his self is one of the many effects of God's power. When God appears unto him by revealing His effect, man becomes aware of his Lord, realising the error of those who say that his self endures from the beginning to the end of his life unchanged. He would also understand the way in which his self endures through the likes. And it follows from remembering his Lord that he forgets his self, since his self is none other than the effect of his Lord's power. So at that moment of remembrance he loses awareness of his self completely. But if his self appears to him not as an effect of his Lord's power but as his self, he would then have remembered his self and forgotten his Lord. In fact, he would have also forgotten himself, as God said: "They forgot God, so He made them forget themselves" (59:19). In any case, man's self remains an effect of his Lord's power, although it can be considered in two respects: in respect of being man's self and in respect of being an effect of his Lord's power. These two considerations contrast one another; they cannot be united from one perspective. When one is recalled, the other is forgotten. Thus, when considering his self, man is reminded: "remember your Lord when you have forgotten" (18:24), that is, when you have forgotten the otherness you are considering when considering yourself. He is also reminded: "And remember your Lord in yourself" (7:205), that is, when you consider yourself so that the other aspect might be revealed to you; the aspect that shows your self being an effect of your Lord's power. This way you would know yourself and you would know your Lord, as it was said: "whosoever knows his self knows his Lord" (*Miftah*, 235–236).

'Abd al-Ghani's critique of self-consciousness resonates with the phenomenologist critique of Cartesian philosophy championed in the twentieth century by Martin Heidegger and Hans-Georg Gadamer. In fact, 'Abd al-Ghani's argument prefigures that of Heidegger in a profound way. Yet even those who upheld a Cartesian position in the Islamic debate, did not conflate the conscious "self" with the conscious "mind." The ego, in other words, was not reducible to reason. Also, the debate in the Islamic context offered no place to reduce human nature to its physiological and psychological components as was the case with the works that emerged in the Enlightenment. Such views remained alien to the Muslim thinkers of the period. And unlike the decentring of humanity in the Enlightenment cosmology, Islamic thinkers protected the centrality of humanity in the cosmic hierarchy both theologically and cosmologically well into the nineteenth century.

RELIGION AND OTHERNESS

With the rethinking of the relationship between God, man, and the world and the emergence of new social and anthropological sciences, a radical paradigm shift in dealing with otherness took place. In medieval and renaissance Europe, Christianity was the horizon on which the difference between the Europeans and non-Europeans was experienced and interpreted. It was religion that enabled the understanding of otherness and provided the criteria for appreciating its worth. "Within the Christian conception of Otherness, anthropology did not exist; there was, rather, demonology. It was in relation to the Fall and to the influence of Sin and Satan that the Other took on his historically specific meaning" (McGrane, 1989, ix). The rise of the science of man in the anthropological sense during the Enlightenment enabled the articulation of a secular conception of self and otherness based on socio-cultural rather than religious values.

The French encyclopaedist Denis Didero, in his contribution to Raynal's *History of the Settlement*, reveals aspects of the shift in perspective from religion to anthropology. Explaining the way in which human equality and difference should be understood, he opened by saying: "Men! You are all brethren. How long will you defer to acknowledge each other? How long will it be before you perceive that nature, your common mother, offers nourishment equally to all her children? Why must you destroy each other; and why must the hand that feeds you be continually stained with blood?"(Hyland *et al*, 2003, 23) Then, while explaining the nature of blackness in black people, he went on to point out the irrationality of traditional Christian theology on this issue:

> [T]heology, after having made a race of men guilty and unfortunate from the fault of Adam; hath made a race of black men, in order to punish the fratricide of his son. The Negroes are the descendent of Cain. If their father was an assassin, it must be allowed that his posterity have made a severe atonement for his crime; and that the descendants of the pacific Abel have thoroughly avenged the innocent blood of their father (Hyland *et al*, 2003, 24).

The European colonial expansion brought about contact with diverse cultures and religions, while the growing interest in human nature brought about an unprecedented curiosity about the ways of life of the non-Europeans. Although Christianity remained a superior religion for the Europeans, it gradually lost its claim to be *the* only true religion. Religious thinking was infused by insights from anthropological studies that tended to interpret religious mysteries and differences in scientific, socio-cultural terms. Thus, during the Enlightenment, "Christianity ceased being the most general coordinating grid from within which and upon which one could both order and account for difference" (McGrane, 1989, 55). As God became disinterested in the daily affairs of humanity, and as Satan mutated into a symbol and Hell into a metaphor, the function of *infidelity* was assumed by *ignorance*, that is, by un-enlightenment, which meant the dwelling in the darkness of one's errors. Difference was accounted for by man's relationship to the enlightening truth that the civilized Europeans had kindled up and took upon themselves to spread among the primitive people around the globe (McGrane, 1989, 56).

During the Enlightenment, the criteria of faith and unbelief, piety and infidelity, gradually lost their relevance in a society concerned more with knowledge, civility, and the light of reason. Knowledge and ignorance, civility and savagery, became the new paradigms that defined otherness and the new horizon upon which encounters with the other were experienced. Reason, the unique character of the human species, was historicized and endowed with a developmental character that progressed in time toward a better understanding of the truth. Superstitions and myths were thus seen as products of ignorant minds and undeveloped reason. Non-Europeans were positioned on a scale according to their distance from and proximity to the Europeans' most advanced and enlightened stage.

Islamic Extremism

In the Islamic context, religion continued to be the main criterion for understanding and dealing with otherness. The continuous dominance of the religious authority had prevented a shift toward anthropology and the prevailing theocentric views disabled the emergence of a new moral code for dealing with otherness. Successive defeats by the Europeans rendered the Muslims more sensitive toward the growing power of the Christian infidels, and made them more defensive in their intellectual exchanges with Europe. In 1697, shaykh al-Islam Fayd Allah wrote to 'Abd al-Ghani from Istanbul, seeking his much needed prayers for the support of the Muslims troops that were going through difficult times in their wars with the Europeans. In response, 'Abd al-Ghani wrote twice, offering his support and calling on all Muslims to stand behind the embattled army of the empire. In this context, the rise of Islamic extremism tended to reassert the superiority of Islam and to entrench the polarity of faith and unbelief as the main criterion for dealing with otherness from within and without the empire.

Contrasting sentiments flared. When Khalifa was advocating for the necessity and utility of science in achieving human happiness and trying to cultivate a rational, open-minded sentiment, his contemporary, Qadizade, was cultivating extremism and provoking violence against mystics and intolerance against mystical beliefs and practices. Between 1621 and 1685, as already mentioned, the Qadizadeli movement wreaked havoc in Istanbul with the Sufis bearing the brunt of their offensive and often bloody attacks. Khalifa was apprehensive about the emerging extremism and warned against its consequences. He called upon the preachers to "gently admonish and advise the people to turn toward the Sunna and to beware of innovations," and pleaded with them not to "spread extremist notions and so provoke the people and sow dissension among the community of Muhammad" (Zilfi, 1986, 251).

Qadizade, the son of a provincial judge of western Anatolia, studied under the rationalist theologian al-Birgili (d. 1573), before moving to Istanbul to pursue a career as a mosque preacher. Al-Birgili was the author of the famous tract *The Muhammadan Way*, on which 'Abd al-Ghani wrote a major commentary. Qadizade's "gifts of expression and grace of delivery" enabled him to rise quickly, giving him access

to the pulpits of the imperial mosques (Zilfi, 1986, 253). In his ser-
mons, he advocated rationalist, puritanical ideas and fundamentalist ethics with the aim of ridding Islam of un-Islamic beliefs and
practices, and especially the innovations of Sufism and popular religion. He directed his attacks specifically against the popular Khalwati
order that was led by Sivasi Efendi (d. 1639). The dispute was centred
on the difference between a law-defined orthodoxy upheld by
Qadizade and his followers, and spirituality-oriented methods of
Sufism. The religious tension in Istanbul spilled over to other
Ottoman cities, and the fundamentalist movement attracted eminent supporters from the provinces, among whom Muhammad
al-Ustuwani (d. 1661) of Damascus was particularly known for the
terror and destruction he inflicted on the Sufis and their lodges.

Although the Qadizadeli movement represented the mood and
sentiment of mosque preachers and not the top official *ulama*, its
longevity, intensity, and wide reach point to the growing intolerance
within Islam during that period. Only a few decades after the demise
of the Qadizadelis, a similar fundamentalist movement, the
Wahhabiyya, emerged in Arabia and had a more lasting effect on the
Muslim world. The Ottoman Empire that was founded on confes-
sional diversity was growing intolerant of religious differences.

Concurrent with the rise of Qadizadeli extremism, the leading
imam of Medina, Ahmad al-Qushashi (d. 1660), revealed an intolerant attitude that concerned 'Abd al-Ghani. Although he was an
important commentator on Sufi works and a transmitter of Ibn
'Arabi's teachings, al-Qushashi seemed unable to share the Sufis'
open-mindedness and ecumenical spirit as represented in the teachings of Ibn 'Arabi and his followers. In his commentary on *The
Universal Man* by the renowned fifteenth-century Sufi 'Abd al-Karim
al-Jili (d. 1428), al-Qushashi dismissed al-Jili's ecumenism that presents all major religions as legitimate forms of worship that are, in
one form or another, grounded in divine unity. He found this as
undermining the superiority of Islam. Reading al-Qushashi's work,
'Abd al-Ghani felt the need to defend Sufi ecumenism and to
re-enforce al-Jili's ideas. He responded to al-Qushashi with a treatise

on the transcendent unity of religions that revealed his life-long struggle with the contrasting perspectives of the truth and the law.

The Truth and the Law

The bitter struggle between the Sufis and their opponents coloured the intellectual climate of the seventeenth and eighteenth centuries and left visible marks on 'Abd al-Ghani's life and works. At the intellectual level, this struggle was expressed in the growing divergence between the approach of the truth and the approach of the law. Very early on in his career, 'Abd al-Ghani revealed a personal struggle with the conflicting demands of his commitment to the universal truths, according to his belief in the Unity of Being, and to the divine law, according to his belief in Islam. In *A Treatise on the Islamic Doctrines ('Aqa'id)*, an early work he wrote at the age of twenty-five shortly after returning from his brief trip to Istanbul, 'Abd al-Ghani attempted to deal with this polarity by articulating a division between the inward and outward aspects of religion. He prefaced his treatise with the following statement:

> This is a collection of what God-most-high has obligated man to do, according to what is possible, of the inward obligation that must be introduced first followed by the outward obligation, which the jurists took upon themselves to explain. It is presented in a great style: I have divided it into two parts, asking God for the right orientation to me and to those seeking guidance along the same path ('Aqa'id, 14).

The two parts of the treatise distinguished between "matters to do with divinity" and "matters to do with prophecy." There is nothing new about the inward-outward and truth-law polarities. Many Sufis before him had worked within, and elaborated on, this complex binary; however, the divinity–prophecy split was a new corollary. God and the Prophet normally side with the truth, but in 'Abd al-Ghani's intriguing division divinity was identified with spirituality and mystical knowledge, while prophecy was relegated to corporeality and knowledge of religious law. This dichotomy grew sharper

and deeper in the following years, acquiring greater magnitude with 'Abd al-Ghani's maturity and spiritual growth.

In his thirties, 'Abd al-Ghani wrote several works that expressed the truth–law polarity. Some focused on the interpretations of the law with regard to specific issues and practices, such as the virtues of Sufi saints, the rituals associated with the veneration of their gravesites and tombs, and the use of musical instruments. Others presented hermeneutical understandings of key religious concepts, such as "sin," "repentance," "belief," "unbelief," "hypocrisy," "polytheism," and so forth. Among the latter works, two were particularly expressive of 'Abd al-Ghani's hermeneutical scope and profound desire to uncover the deeper meanings or the inner truth of things. The first was *The Lordly Opening and the Compassionate Effusion (Fath)*, which he wrote at the age of thirty-five; the second, *The Wine of Longing and the Tune of Melodies (Han)*, came three years later as an extended commentary on a famous mystical treatise by a celebrated Damascene Sufi known as shaykh Arislan.

The Lordly Opening, in both its scope of interpretation and its style of exposition, reveals Ibn 'Arabi's strong influence on 'Abd al-Ghani. In his introduction, he expressed his fear of being misunderstood by the guardians of the law along with those "who had become impure by the sins' smoke screen, of which they are unaware while being preoccupied with the demands of nature" (*Fath*, 7). Following Ibn 'Arabi and the Sufi tradition, 'Abd al-Ghani maintained that all things, physical and conceptual, have hidden secrets with which the science of truth is concerned. These hidden secrets enable us to understand the true meanings of things and consequently broaden our interpretations of the law. For example, "sin," according to the law, is being in *discordance* with God with regard to His delivered message. In reality, however, "sin" is being in *concordance* with God with regard to his creation. The Arabic word for "sin," *dhanb*, signifies "otherness." In 'Abd al-Ghani's hermeneutics, "sin" takes on, first, a positive meaning with reference to God's intention of founding otherness, and, second, a negative meaning with reference to God's preferences (expressed through the law) once otherness is founded (*Fath*, 9–29).

In *The Wine of Longing*, 'Abd al-Ghani shows how Sufi hermeneutics underpin the spiritual approach that focuses on the universal truths. He uses shaykh Arislan's synopsis to articulate in detail the difference between the approach of the truth and the approach of the law. He sees both approaches to be complementary of one another: one, the law, is restrictive "with limits and directions," the other, the truth, is expansive "without limits and directions" (*Han*, 64/130). The "law," *shari'a* in Arabic, means a "source of water." It is so named, 'Abd al-Ghani explains, "because when the community feels thirsty it comes to it to quench its thirst" (*Han*, 64). In other words, the law serves an earthly need, unlike the truth that acts as a mirror in which humanity sees itself. The "truth," *haqiqa* in Arabic, means "the essence of a thing": its immutable reality in itself and not what one renders of this reality in one's own understanding, which is necessarily conditioned by one's capacity and predisposition. One can only understand what one's horizon reveals, he adds, and not the reality of the thing that stands as a mirror in which one sees one's own limitations (*Han*, 65). Thus, the masters of the law, being limited in their understanding, cannot embrace the science of the truth, whereas the expansive horizon of the masters of the truth can encompass that of the law. He explains:

> The master of the science of truth uncovers the truths only without denying the science of divine law, whereas the master of the science of divine law rules with what he knows of the divine law's rulings, but without knowing the realities of things or knowing God's revelations in them. So he misses out on the universal unity, which presupposes discerning the presence of God-most-high in everything, isolating himself with a disguised polytheism while letting forgetfulness overtakes his heart. Thus, you see him the more he exaggerates in the strictness of applying God's rulings on himself and on others, the more disguised polytheist and distant from God he becomes without him noticing (*Bayan*).

The complex polarity of the truth and the law remained one of the core issues that preoccupied 'Abd al-Ghani throughout his life. His reflections on its implications permeated many of his works. At the age of seventy-eight, he wrote a treatise titled *The Imams' Excuse in Guiding the Community ('Uzr)*, revealing his ongoing preoccupation with this issue. He introduced the treatise, saying: "This is a treatise I wrote in order to reconcile between the scholars of the divine law and the established masters among the scholars of truth, who deal with obscure and transcendental issues" (*'Uzr*, 147). The treatise shows that his perspective and position had by then shifted onto more reconciliatory grounds. He was also careful to point out, though indirectly, that not all those who spoke in the name of the truth were genuine masters, and to appear as taking an objective position in addressing the scholars from both camps.

Transcendent Unity of Religions

In the last chapter of his widely circulated work, *The Universal Man*, al-Jili articulated his philosophy of religion, expanding many of the ideas that Ibn 'Arabi had introduced. He attempted to explain, in some rational terms, the basis for religious differences and the reason for the superiority of Islam. He argued for the transcendent unity of religions, explaining that all religions are but different pathways leading to the same end, and that all people worship—by necessity and providence, not by choice—one and the same God. To maintain the superiority of Islam, however, al-Jili presented an interesting analysis of ten different religious dogmas from the Islamic perspective, which he, of course, upheld to be the best pathway to follow. Al-Jili's ecumenical perspective did not impress the jurists, prompting the leading scholar of Medina, Ahmad al-Qushashi, who was known as "the *imam* of the believers in the Unity of Being" (*Khulasat*, 1:345), to write a commentary dismissing his claims.

Disturbed by al-Qushashi's views, 'Abd al-Ghani responded with *The Disclosure and Clarification of the Secrets of Religions (Bayan)*. In this text he criticized al-Qushashi's misunderstanding, clarified al-Jili's intentions, and articulated his own approach to the philosophy of religions. The main question that underlined this work was how to resolve the conflicting demands of the ecumenism of the Unity of Being with the exclusivity of the Islamic faith. One is rational, demanding an egalitarian and inclusive understanding; the other is dogmatic, demanding a discriminatory and exclusive attitude.

The egalitarian, inclusive understanding derives from the universality of the science of truth, the core of the Unity of Being, which, according to 'Abd al-Ghani, is expressed in the equitable relationship Being bares to all beings, be they essences, attributes, states, or deeds of every creature in the absolute sense, or be they spirits, souls, bodies, forms, meanings, quick-passing thoughts, or conceptions, whether of human, angelic, or jinni source, in the outward or the inward worlds, and be they of the creatures we know and are able to perceive or those we do not. Thus, from the ecumenical, universal perspective of the Unity of Being, all beings (or creatures) necessarily have an equal relationship to Being, the very foundation of their existence. In this respect, 'Abd al-Ghani asserts, "all are on the straight path and right in their states, speeches, and deeds, because they are all, in this regard, the acts of the most high and the traces of his most beautiful names" (*Bayan*).

By contrast, all world religions present discriminatory views upon which they predicate their claims for exclusive ownership of salvation and exclusive entitlement to God's special favours. From the perspective of religious law, God projects certain preferences: He favours certain people overs others, values certain religions more than others, enjoins people to do certain things, and prohibits them from doing others. The law by its very specific and discriminatory nature contrasts the universal equality inherent in the nature of Being.

The ecumenical perspective of the transcendent unity of religions tends to undermine the core discriminatory and exclusivist elements that all religions have, by necessity, inherent in their belief systems in order to maintain the credibility of their exclusive promise for, and access to, salvation. Islam was no exception. This was, partly at least, the main reason behind al-Qushashi's dismissive response. But Sufis in general, and Ibn 'Arabi's school in particular, tend to rise above the apparent contradiction and search for modes of understanding that accommodate both positions. Ibn 'Arabi, for example, saw love as both the cause of creation and the enduring bond that connects all creatures to their creator. He regarded all kinds of worship as genuine expressions of love: "The creatures have believed in God in many different ways," he openly wrote, "and I believe in all of what they have believed in" (*Fath*, 45). In the famous lines he wrote in *The Interpreter of Desires (Tarjuman)*, Ibn 'Arabi boldly declared:

> My heart has become capable of every form,
>> it is a pasture for the gazelles and a convent for the Christian monks.
> And a temple for idols and a Ka'ba for the pilgrim,
>> and tablets for the Tora and parchments for the Qur'an.
> I follow the religion of love, whatever way
>> its caravan may go, for love is my religion and my faith
>> (*Tarjuman*, 19).

From Islam's dogmatic perspective, such a view tends to blur the differences between religions, to marginalize the necessity and function of the law, and, most importantly, to undermine the superiority of Islam over other religions. To address these concerns, 'Abd al-Ghani had to introduce some unconventional ideas. First, he argued that the Islamic faith was revealed to the Prophet Muhammad in two complimentary parts: one communicated the truth, the other dictated the law. While maintaining that there was no exclusion or contradiction between the two parts, he argued for the autonomy of each part with regard to its function and logic. This was necessary in order to overcome the contradiction that appears once the same logic is applied to both sides. To explain the rationale of his polarity, 'Abd al-Ghani cited two Qur'anic statements: one says that God grants wisdom to whoever He wants, the other dictates that God's ruling must not be questioned. The first implies that whoever is enlightened by divine wisdom rises above diversity to see the inner unity that binds all religions; whereas the second implies that the discriminatory divine law that negates the equality among different religions cannot be viewed from the same perspective and must not be questioned. In other words, the enlightening divine wisdom, while enabling one to understand the inner meanings of difference, does not—by the empowerment of such an enlightenment—qualify one to question divine discrimination.

Accordingly, 'Abd al-Ghani restricted the science of truth to dealing with the creatures' relationship to God, the universal process of their manifestation, the realities that govern their existence, and the divine revelations that ensure their adherence to God. He presented it as the science of "disclosure and visualization," whereby one knows the difference between the worshiper and the worshiped, achieves inner purification of one's heart, seeks knowledge of the unknown, and uncovers the divine order in the universe. It is the science of the transcendental divine presence whose sole purpose is to explore and understand the realities of Being.

Thus viewed, the science of truth has nothing to do with the merits of peoples' beliefs, convictions, and obligations, or with the divine ruling and prohibition, or with the interpretations of the divine injunctions. These were relegated to the science of the law that is concerned with the conditions of beings. The law allows us to know what pious deeds are, what obedience and disobedience, faith and unbelief, right and wrong are, and what they entail in terms of divine satisfaction and wrath. Consequently, all beings, according to 'Abd al-Ghani, must be considered from two different perspectives: one with regard to God, the other with regard to the world. With regard to God, all beings, including humans, are "on the straight path and right in their states, speeches, and deeds," because in this respect they are none other than God's acts and the traces of his most beautiful names. With regard to their worldly existence, however, not everyone is on the straight path. Humans are endowed with free will and power, whereby they project choices concerning what God allows and prohibits. In this respect, some are on the straight path while others are not, some are right while others are wrong, some are faithful while others are infidels.

'Abd al-Ghani's ecumenism involves some inconsistent logic in its rationalization of religious differences. According to the logic of the truth God is ecumenical, but according to the logic of the law He is discriminatory. This is expressed in His names and attributes. He is at once the one-who-guides and one-who-misguides. In themselves, the two names are equal in beauty and transcendence, 'Abd al-Ghani asserts, but in their applications they discriminate between the guided faithful, with whom God is pleased, and the misguided infidels, with whom God is angry. As a result, some groups are eventually rewarded while others are punished. He further explains that the name the one-who-guides is necessarily expressed in the Islamic faith only, while the one-who-misguides is expressed in all other religions. As to why this is so, 'Abd al-Ghani cites the verse: "God rules; no one questions his ruling" (13:41).

If guidance and misguidance are the traces of God's most beautiful names, and satisfaction and wrath are their consequent attributes, and if all are inherently good, and if God the most perfect and beautiful produces nothing other than beauty and perfection, how then can His preference for Islam and apparently prejudiced rulings with regard to other religions be explained? This question involves a crossing between the two autonomous domains 'Abd al-Ghani had set up, a move he did not take, heeding the call not to question the unquestionable. This is where the attitude of Muslim thinkers differed from that of their European contemporaries, who were prepared to tear down the barrier of religious reverence and to question the unquestionable.

In mapping the truth-law division over the Being-beings polarity, 'Abd al-Ghani was able to accommodate an ecumenical dimension, however limited its horizon might have been. By separating the dealing with the realities of Being, the realm of the truth, from the dealing with the conditions of beings, the realm of the law, 'Abd al-Ghani was at least able to create a space of philosophical reasoning outside the disabling religious prejudice of faith and unbelief. This rendered him receptive to new ideas and novelties as can be seen in the legal opinions he issued to allow the smoking of tobacco, the drinking of coffee, and the use of musical instruments, as well as in his repeated advice to religious clerics to refrain from accusing others of infidelity.

Islam as Natural Faith

Within the broad framework of his philosophy of religion, 'Abd al-Ghani's specific thought on religious otherness can be found in two works. One is a commentary on a famous poem by a mystic known as al-Shushtari (d. 1269), who presents his mystical ideas in bold Christian imageries; the other is an extended rebuttal of a criticism by a Turkish scholar of the views of both Ibn 'Arabi and 'Abd al-Ghani on God's treatment of followers of other religions. Both works reveal that although there was no shift from the medieval perspective that projected Islam as the dominant horizon against which otherness was interpreted and appreciated, 'Abd al-Ghani was committed to the ecumenical approach of Ibn 'Arabi and al-Jili.

Abu al-Hasan al-Shushtari of Islamic Spain was a student of the renowned philosopher and mystic Ibn Sab'in (d. 1269/71). He wrote several works on mystical science but is best known for his poetry. In an interesting short poem of twenty-nine lines, he described a visit to a convent and an encounter with Christian monks. It opens with the following lines:

> Be courteous at the door of the convent and take off your shoes,
>   and salute the monks and stay over with them.
> And esteem in it the priest if you desire a special attention,
>   and respect the deacon if you want to be highly regarded.
> Before you are the voices of the choir, listen
>   to them, yet beware not to let them steal your mind (*Muftari*, 225).

The poem attracted condemnation from some jurists and 'Abd al-Ghani was called upon to provide a commentary that reveals the hidden meanings of al-Shushtari's metaphors. The main challenge the poem had posed was how to interpret the Christian imageries in a positive light but without lending credence to Christianity itself. To do so, 'Abd al-Ghani presented a two-sided argument: one focused on the universality of the Islamic faith, the other on the unified nature of the mystical experience. He argued that Islam was the most universal of all religions and that the approaches of Muslim saints, according to their personal inclinations, were often coloured with other religions that were subsumed within the embracing perspective of Islam. He also argued that since the mystical experience was unified in nature, it transcended the linguistic expressions and tangible imageries of different religions. This way he was able to go beyond the literal meanings of al-Shushtari's expressions, to explain the legitimacy of his experience, and to reassert the superiority of Islam. Christianity, from this perspective, was legitimized but only as a specific expression of the universality of the Islamic faith. In their own religious beliefs and practices, however, the Christians remained infidels. "The Muslims are more deserving of the association with Jesus son of Mary than the Christians," he wrote, "because they are infidels, disbelieving in the truth of his message. Their way is based on ignorance and obstinacy, while the Muslims believe in him and in the truth he delivered through his message" (*Muftari*, 225).

Elsewhere, 'Abd al-Ghani elaborated his perspective on the universality of the Islamic faith, presenting a hermeneutical understanding of faith and unbelief in terms of nature and concealment. Everyone is born with a natural faith, he says; people are faithful by nature and the natural faith is, of course, Islam. But sometimes, this nature becomes concealed with misguided concepts and false beliefs that turn one into an "infidel," *kafir* in Arabic, from *kufr*, "infidelity," which literally means "concealment." Hence the farmer is called *kafir*, he adds, because he conceals the seeds in the ground. Accordingly, "infidelity" becomes "the concealment of faith." And since faith is an inherent attribute of the human nature, one needs to make no onerous efforts to unveil it even when one has been sidetracked by other beliefs. Once those misguided beliefs are removed, faith would naturally emerge in its place as it ever was (*Fath*, 74).

To illustrate this idea, 'Abd al-Ghani uses a scientific example, comparing faith and unbelief to the attractive force inherent in a magnet that is being blocked by a holding hand. Once the hand is removed the magnet performs its natural attractive function. This is how unbelief works: it conceals one's natural goodness with false ideas. As for the consequences of one's infidelity and the nature of one's suffering, he adopts Ibn 'Arabi's radical interpretation that all suffering will eventually transform into degrees of pleasure that match one's status in piety. Ibn 'Arabi plays on the etymological meaning of "suffering," *'azab* in Arabic, to argue that at the end of an assigned period of punishment the infidel's suffering will convert into "pleasure," *'uzuba* (*Fath*, 77–78).

Language and Ethnicity

In addition to their rather charitable view towards the unbelievers, both Ibn 'Arabi and 'Abd al-Ghani had also argued that it was possible for God to go back on his threat to punish them, and that Christians, Jews, and followers of other religions were entitled to eternal happiness. These views attracted harsh criticism from a Turkish scholar to whom 'Abd al-Ghani addressed a lengthy, scornful rebuttal titled *A Response to the One who Spoke about Ibn al-'Arabi* (*Radd*). In this response, 'Abd al-Ghani extended the debate beyond the religious issues in question into ethnicity, which he linked to religious virtues. The text reveals a prejudiced attitude towards the Turks based on the firm belief in the superiority of the Arabs and their language (Winter, 1988). "It is most wondrous," he wrote, "that there has arisen in the lands of the Turks a man, from the deserts' boors and the steppes' impure ones, so keen on accusing an Arab, son of an Arab (referring to Ibn 'Arabi), of infidelity and he is an ill foreigner, son of a foreigner, even though the Arabs are the lords of both the foreigners and the Turks as is commonly known and established among the *ulama*. It is the Arabs who brought the Turks into Islam" (*Radd*, 54).

Following these prejudiced remarks, 'Abd al-Ghani presented a lengthy argument on how, according to both reason and tradition, the Arabs were superior to the Turks and other ethnic groups. The basis of this superiority was not racial but intellectual and derives primarily from the strength of the Arabic language. "There is no doubt," he asserted, "that the Arabs are most transparent in rationality and most clear in expression, and that their tongue is the most perfect in the exposition and elucidation of meanings … And since this is confirmed of their language, their intellects are known to be

the most perfect, because the tongue is a translator of what is intel-
lectualized" (*Radd*, 55). It is for this reason, he further argued, that
"unlike the non-Arabs, the Arab minds were not in need of training,
to comprehend meanings and sciences, with a rational instrument,
the function of which is to prevent the mind from error, the one
known as the science of logic" (*Radd*, 55).

This work of 'Abd al-Ghani, which he wrote at the age of fifty-
three, is important for several reasons. It adds another dimension to
his philosophy of religion, ecumenical perspective, and tolerant
views on religious otherness. It also reveals aspects of the ethnic sen-
sitivity between the Arabs and other Muslim groups, mainly the
Turks and the Persians, and the sense of superiority the Arabs had felt
because of their language. But most importantly, perhaps, is the indirect reference to the emphasis the Persians placed on logic and rational sciences in contrast to the emphasis the Arabs placed on
literature, poetry, and linguistic sciences. It is no coincidence, therefore, that one of the most eminent contemporaries of 'Abd al-Ghani
is the great Persian philosopher Sadr al-Din al-Shirazi (d. 1641).

'Abd al-Ghani's views on, and attitude toward, otherness show
that faith and dogma had remained the main ground of reasoning
about religious and ethnic difference. Yet, his sophisticated explanations reflected an implicit demand to expand the rational scope of
religious reasoning. In his world at least, there was a space constructive enough for Christian friends to seek his insights on theological
issues and for him to describe them as "brothers in abstract thought,
whose noble souls and subtle selves have become moons in the sky of
unity" (*Jawab*).

THE EMERGENCE OF THE PUBLIC

The intellectual developments during the Enlightenment resulted in
a rapid secularization of the society that in turn led to significant
changes at the socio-cultural and government-state levels. The emergence of the public as a space of communication, a domain where

important issues affecting society were exposed, debated, and judged was one of the main hallmarks of this period. This was enabled by a burgeoning print culture that provided an important medium for members of the public to express and communicate their opinions. New institutions of public sociality that developed in tandem with the public sphere included coffee houses, salons, and Masonic lodges (Melton, 2003). The public sphere as a cultural and political arbiter grew in importance to occupy a central role in the emerging civil society. The emerging authority of the public was critical in marginalizing religious authority and in breaking its monopoly over the truth. The sense of secularity that underpinned the prosperity of the nascent public space depended on the growing credibility of secular sciences.

The rise of the public sphere was associated historically with two long-term developments. First was the rise of modern nation-states, a process whereby the society, as the realm of private interest and activity, became distinct from the state that represented the sphere of public power. Second was the rise of capitalism that further disjointed state and society. With the growing autonomy and self-awareness of society, through trade and development-focused culture, national and international markets expanded and communication networks grew wider and denser. This in turn affected the family and household domain, which transformed as the market gradually replaced the household as a primary domain of production. In the eighteenth century, the family and household transformed from a sphere of social necessity and patriarchal dominance into "a sphere of intimacy and affection" (Melton, 2003).

The public sphere derived its efficacy at both the political and intellectual levels from three characteristics. First, it gave credibility to the dictates of reason—as the ultimate arbiter in debates—over the authority and identity of the participants. Second, it provided no protection or immunity from criticism to anything or anyone; everything was considered to be democratically available for scrutiny. Third, it almost by default displayed natural hostility toward secrecy and a dismissive attitude toward mysteries, since publicity was the primary character of the public sphere. But for the public to be able to engage effectively in the public sphere, it, first, had to be informed, and, second, had to have a medium for public expression and communication. This provided new possibilities for the burgeoning print culture that produced newspapers and magazines as new media of mass communication (Melton, 2003).

The use of reason in public created an audience-oriented subjectivity that was less reliant on dogmatic belief and unquestionable individual authority than on reasoned argumentation and collective and institutional authority. All claims of truth had to make sense to audiences made up of individuals with diverse backgrounds and competing interests. This has since significantly changed the modes of exercising power and authority in the European society.

Engaging the Public

The Qadizadeli experience in Istanbul revealed sustained efforts to cultivate public sentiment in order to exercise a new form of religious authority. The Qadizadeli preachers were not members of the *ulama* hierarchy but rather of lower ranked group of scholars with modest education, achievements, and career expectations. They thus did not enjoy the same level of authority as the professors of law, who were not always sympathetic to their fundamentalist approach. Unlike the *ulama*, however, the preachers had a stronger connection with the urban public and were closer to them in their personal circumstances and living conditions. The Qadizadeli preachers were aware of their limitations and relied on the power of the public to drive their cause. They were effective public speakers, attuned to the values of their audiences, and keen to engage the public in contemporary issues affecting their lives. Through that they were able to spread their ideas, to generate wide anti-mystical sentiment, and to mobilize the public against the Sufis.

Alongside this religiously charged, volatile public sphere there were other types of peaceful public activities. The coffee houses appeared in Arab and Ottoman cities long before they did in Europe. They first appeared in Damascus in 1534 but were banned in 1546 in response to the legal decrees issued by several local jurists. Shortly after, however, they were officially authorized by the Ottomans and rapidly multiplied. They reached Istanbul in 1555 "on the initiative of a 'wag called Shams,' an inhabitant of Damascus" (Degeorge, 2004, 176). The battle over the legality of coffee drinking and smoking continued during 'Abd al-Ghani's life and he himself weighed into the debate in favour of both.

Another semi-public, elitist sphere that grew in parallel with the coffee-drinking culture facilitated recreational activities, entertainment, and cultural exchanges. Senior government officials and distinguished religious personalities joined members of elite families and notables in regular gatherings in private and public gardens for entertainment and poetic exchanges. These became common features of urban life in the Ottoman capital as well as in provincial centres like Damascus. They provided a forum for cultured social exchange. 'Abd al-Ghani, as we saw earlier, rose to fame in these gatherings and remained committed to participating in them throughout his life. His anthology of poems *The Wine of Babel and the Singing of Nightingales (Khamrat)* is a valuable record of some of these social events. It presents interesting images of Damascus urbanity, landscape, and social practices. In these gatherings women were absent: they were not family picnics, but rather, men only outings. The absence of women, however, was compensated for by the amatory elegies and love poetry that often mapped the feminine virtues of the beloved over the landscape. The appreciation of nature's beauty was mediated by poetic imageries celebrating femininity and revealing men's effeminate languishing character that was often concealed in the presence of women (*Khamrat*).

On the opposite side of this exclusive semi-public space, there was the all inclusive public forum associated with the yearly pilgrimage caravans. Massive congregations used to assemble in Damascus and Cairo before setting out on a return trip to Mecca and Medina that took about five to six months. In this yearly event, a wide range of social and cultural groups met and exchanged ideas and thoughts over a considerably long period of time. In this mobile forum of intellectual exchange, ideas spread fast, masters debated important issues, and students studied with their admired masters and received licences to teach.

Despite their religious and social efficacy, these public forums did not give birth to a politicized public sphere similar to the one that emerged in Europe. This was mainly because, first, individual author- ity—religious and political—continued to dominate, and, second, the nascent print culture received a hostile response from religious authorities and was immaturely aborted. Because of the sacred char- acter of the Arabic script, there was a strong resistance to mechanical printing in the Ottoman and Arab world. The press founded in Aleppo in 1706 did not succeed, while the Muteferriqa Press founded in Istanbul in 1729 operated intermittently, and folded in 1794. It produced only a handful of publications, twenty-three titles in total. The venture was completely foreign: the press came from France, the typefaces from Holland, and the personnel from Austria. There was not enough momentum, intensity of activities, and support for the new print culture to survive and for new forms of mass communication to make an impact. Newspapers, journals, and magazines did not appear until the nineteenth century.

Unprecedented Exposure

In his biographical account, al-Baytamani described how 'Abd al- Ghani presided over many public readings of Ibn 'Arabi's controver- sial text *The Meccan Revelations* (*al-Futuhat al-Makkiyya*) at the Selimiyya mosque, around the author's grave. It is not clear from al- Baytamani's notes what the public readings involved and in what forms they were conducted, but it is likely that selected students were assigned to reading the text in successive instalments while 'Abd al-Ghani expounded and explained the meanings publicly. "This was unprecedented," al-Baytamani wrote, "no one has done it before, since this divine science used to be read in secret, while he read it in public because of his strong intention and highly esteemed knowledge" (*Mashrab*, 9). Considering that the text is over

3000 pages in single-spaced, tight format, one can imagine how many sessions it would have taken 'Abd al-Ghani to go though even selected parts. And considering that mystical sciences in general, and the works of Ibn 'Arabi in particular, were normally read in private Sufi sessions, one can also imagine how exciting and unsettling 'Abd al-Ghani's novel presentations were. Al-Baytamani noted that the sessions were very popular, attracting an unusually mixed social group that included notables, religious clerics, scholars, judges, and governors as well as mystics and lay people. People came from other towns to attend the sessions, he added. Al-Baytamani himself was unsure about the merit of such a rather excessive exposure of mystical knowledge in public, and commented somewhat hesitantly on his master's performance. Yet, he admitted that it was a novel practice that "no one could disprove and challenge him on because of the great lucidity and eloquence of his discourse" (Mashrab, 9).

The nature of intellectual exchange in public is, as already mentioned, different from that in private. Unlike his elitist private classes, 'Abd al-Ghani, in the public sessions, would have had to communicate complex ideas to an audience of varying levels of intelligence and allegiance. He would have had to rely less on his own authority and convictions, still much less on Ibn 'Arabi's, and more on his rational explanations. His ultimate aim would not be to enlighten a few individuals sharing his conviction, but to create an informed audience with an adequate level of knowledge and rationality to be able to engage with, communicate, and appreciate the merit of the ideas being discussed. The novelty of the experience generated mixed feelings of excitement and unease. People were unsure how to interact with and react to such unprecedented disclosure. Describing the response of a concerned friend, al-Baytamani wrote:

> Once a man told me: "shaykh 'Abd al-Ghani should not have revealed these divine sciences among the public, nor should he have allowed the reading to be publicly heard, because he is the imam of the era, whom the public would follow in matters they do not understand, and because of him they might fall in what is religiously prohibited" (Mashrab, 9–10).

Al-Baytamani shared this feeling, which seemed to have been representative of the general public's reaction to 'Abd al-Ghani's presentations. Though intrigued to share the experience, the Damascenes were confused. Trained to follow religious authorities, they suddenly found themselves being asked to think for themselves and take responsibility for judging the merit of what they were hearing. Even al-Baytamani, with his intimate acquaintance with 'Abd al-Ghani, was doubtful about the merit of his master's intentions. He had a tacit desire to know why 'Abd al-Ghani went public with mystical knowledge; why he stripped it from its elitist, exclusive character; and what he was hoping to achieve. But he lacked the courage to ask. One day, after hearing people's concerns, al-Baytamani went to see his master who was able to sense his disciple's tacit doubts. He advised him not to care about people's criticism and explained that he had no say in whether or not to do what he had done, because he was acting under "the demand of disclosure." And with his spontaneous, poetic manner, he reassured his concerned disciple:

> They say: do not utter with what you know
>> amongst the ignorant folks, for that is shameful.
> I say to them: leave the blame, for we are
>> under the demand of disclosure and the distance is near.
> We have drunk and poured out onto the earth a sip,
>> and the earth, from the glass of the bountiful nobles, must have a
>> share (*Mashrab*, 10).

Rational Disclosure

The demand of "disclosure" (*tajalli*) was 'Abd al-Ghani's stated reason for his public readings of the highly esoteric and controversial mystical text. But what does this really mean? *Tajalli* is a common Sufi term that refers to a range of psychic, intellectual, and spiritual experiences, such as flashes of ideas, intellectual impulses, mystical visions, quick-passing thoughts (*khawatir*), inspirational understandings, and so forth, which are believed to be from a source other than one's own reason. In Sufi terms, *tajalli* is what the lights of the unseen unveil to the hearts. The Sufis use this term particularly to distinguish their intellectual experiences from those of the philosophers who rely on methodical reasoning. There are numerous Sufi texts that document such mystical experiences, which are sometimes expressed in obscure, metaphorical expressions. 'Abd al-Ghani has his own mystical disclosures, the most famous of which was his dialogue with God, cited earlier, that al-Baytamani compared to those of al-Niffari (d. 965) and al-Jilani (d. 1166).

The spiritual impulses that impelled 'Abd al-Ghani to conduct the public readings of mystical texts must have been somewhat different from those that inspired him to privately converse with God. In the former experience, his revelatory impulses would be more like flashes of ideas and quick-passing thoughts, whereas in the latter they would be more like mystical visions and inspirational understanding. In both cases, however, 'Abd al-Ghani claimed that he was not acting voluntarily according to his own whims and desires but rather responding to the impulses he had received from divine sources. Although we can only speculate about the nature of such impulses, his colourful character can provide some insights into his actions.

'Abd al-Ghani was a person with contrasting tendencies, who found pleasures in both material and spiritual worlds. Taking this into account would help us understand what he meant by "the demand of disclosure." After quoting in full 'Abd al-Ghani's famous dialogue with God to emphasize the profundity of his mystical experience, al-Baytamani described his gentle, affable, and reverent character as well as his strictness in observing religious duties and etiquettes of the law. Then he said:

> And it is of his character that he wears splendid cloths, eats delicious food, and sleeps on expensive furniture, without any of these distracting him from God. And when he goes out, he rides on a couch, wearing a headgear in the manner of the distinguished *ulama*, with servants and students walking in front of him and on his right and left sides. He passes by no Muslim without saluting him first with a smiling and cheerful face (*Mashrab*, 35–36).

'Abd al-Ghani also smoked and drank coffee and wrote on the legality of these new emerging habits at a time when they were under strong attacks from conservative jurists. He also delighted in picnics and public entertainments and compiled a large anthology of poems that he composed in those events. This lavish, indulgent lifestyle is clearly not in keeping with traditional Sufi teachings, and his biographers were at pains to show that these anomalies in his character did not contradict or undermine the image of the great Sufi saint they were trying to paint. But 'Abd 'Al-Ghani's personality was difficult to fit within such a stereotypical mould; he was radically different. Through his works, he comes across more as a spiritually inspired rational scholar with poetic sensibility than as an esoteric Sufi saint. His sources of inspirations were, to some extent, "rational disclosures" that engage human reason to interrogate religious truths.

Although 'Abd al-Ghani spoke and wrote profusely about the limitations of human reason, his mystical sensibility is evidently more rational than that of the classical masters, such as al-Niffari, Ibn 'Arabi, al-Jilani and al-Jili, with whom he was often compared. His writings are more methodical and comprehensible than theirs. Even in his most esoteric expressions, his thoughts read as snippets of philosophical reasoning or rationalization of mystical ideas and experiences. For instance, in the dialogue with God quoted above, 'Abd al-Ghani presents a philosophical reasoning about being, non-being, and human mediation cast in the form of mystical exchange. The dialogue form of his reflections might give them a mystical feel, but the subject of the dialogue and its details reveal coherent philosophical reasoning. Such a dialogue could have taken place between a teacher and a disciple, and could simply represent some private reflections on the philosophical notions of being and non-being. With this in mind, "the demand of disclosure" that drove him to publicize mystical knowledge can be understood as the urge of his personal reflections.

'Abd al-Ghani's unprecedented move might have been motivated by a desire to show that there was nothing secretive, unlawful, or un-Islamic about Sufism and Sufi knowledge, nor about the teachings of the most controversial of all, Ibn 'Arabi. Yet, the move had created a new social space for understanding and negotiating mystical knowledge, one wherein mystical ideas were openly discussed and debated. Wittingly or unwittingly, 'Abd al-Ghani adopted the same tactic the Qadizadeli preachers used to provoke the public against Sufism. His sessions aimed at engaging and educating the public, with the intention of cultivating an informed public opinion in support of Sufism. He wanted to dispel the secrecy that had shrouded the mystical path and its sciences for centuries and was used against the Sufis by their opponents. It was a move to rationalize the understanding of mystical ideas.

HIS LEGACY

A View from a Distance

DEPARTING DAMASCUS

In 1706, a big fight broke up in Damascus involving Turkish soldiers and a group of Arab nobles. The soldiers assaulted and abused the nobles and murdered one of them in front of 'Abd al-Ghani's house. 'Abd al-Ghani was enraged by the incident, cursed the Turks, and cried for an end to their cruelty and oppression. For over sixty years he had lived in his parents' place in the Perfume Sellers' market near the Umayyad mosque, but after this incident he decided to abandon the city and move to the foothills of Qasiyun to settle in proximity to Ibn 'Arabi's tomb. He first built a house of rammed earth near the cemetery where shaykh Mahmud, who predicted his birth, used to live. In this remote location, he deserted people for a while until 1707, when he acquired a piece of land in the foothill suburb of al-Salihiyya, overlooking the old city of Damascus, a short walk from the tomb of Ibn 'Arabi. He built a large house there and settled with his family until the end of his life.

The move did not mark any significant shift in 'Abd al-Ghani's interests or in his religious and intellectual preoccupations. He continued to write discursively on the same range of topics according to personal and social demands. Shortly before the incident that triggered his move, 'Abd al-Ghani completed his four-volume commentary on al-Baydawi's interpretation of the Qur'an, which was then

Figure 3.1 A view of the internal courtyard of 'Abd al-Ghani's house after several renovations. The room above the arched space is his room, which is rendered directly inaccessible (author).

one of the most respected and widely consulted texts. This was his last major interpretive study, as all subsequent works were shorter and generally issue-related. Shortly after he moved into the new house in al-Salihiyya, he wrote a poem celebrating God's ninety-nine most beautiful names.

In 1712, he responded to a series of theological questions concerned with divinity and humanity, which were sent to him by some Christians whom he described as "brothers in abstract thought" (*Jawab*). In this period, 'Abd al-Ghani continued to reflect on the concept of Unity of Being, and in 1716 he wrote an extended commentary on *The Presented Gift*, a famous Sufi tract on the topic by an early seventeenth-century mystic of Indian origin.

In the latter part of his life, 'Abd al-Ghani appeared more gracious, benevolent, and magnanimous. The waves of rejection and attacks had receded and he entertained high esteem, wide recognition, and great popularity. His presence was of a royal status, always attracting large audiences. Al-Ghazzi described a public gathering that took place in 1727, three years before 'Abd al-Ghani's death, as being a great feast that lasted for three days and was attended by all Damascene dignitaries, religious authorities, government officials, soldiers, and a large local crowd. Fifty bounds of coffee were brought to serve and entertain the participants (*Wird*, 41). One year earlier, in 1726, 'Abd al-Ghani had a unique, demountable, timber pavilion constructed for him, which was in the form of a large room with windows and a book case raised above a protected space. The installation and dismantling of this pavilion was enabled by specially designed metal hinges, and the whole structure used to be carted to the parks around Damascus on the back of ten mules provided by some of 'Abd al-Ghani's close friends. In that large gathering, 'Abd al-Ghani's pavilion was installed on the bank of the Barada River, wherein he sat "as a king; all were at his service, the leaders and the public, and all the singers, the skilful musicians, and entertainers of Damascus gathered there in a state of utmost cheerfulness and rejoice" (*Wird*, 41).

'Abd al-Ghani remained in good shape until the illness that led to his death at the age of ninety-three (according to the Muslim calendar). He was able to read and write well until the end of his life. He died peacefully in 1731 (on 24 of Sha'ban in the year 1143 of the Muslim calendar) and was mourned by the people of Damascus, which closed down on the day of his funeral. A huge crowd flocked to his house to bid farewell to their beloved master. He was buried according to his will in a domed pavilion he had built in the garden of his house. The place of his residence was later developed into a centre for religious learning, and it has continued to function as such under the patronage of his posterity until the present day.

Figure 3.2 A view of the main entrance of 'Abd al-Ghani's complex in the suburb of al-Salihiyya taken from the minaret (author).

'Abd al-Ghani married twice and had three children, one son Isma'il from his first wife Musliha, whom he divorced during his depression and retreat period, and two daughters, Zaynab and Tahira, from his second wife 'Alma. Zaynab was an eccentric woman, known for her intimidating presence and fearless confrontations with governors and top officials. When she said that her father would not be buried in his pavilion but next to his father in the public cemetery no one could object. It happened, however, that she took a nap while the body was being prepared for burial so the family hurriedly buried him in the pavilion before she woke up. For an unknown reason, she was stabbed to death at the age of seventy-four (*Wird*, 198).

Tahira, 'Abd al-Ghani's youngest daughter, was closely attached to her father. While on his death bed, 'Abd al-Ghani called her and said: "I am leaving and want to take you with me." Zaynab overheard the conversation and thought her father was planning a picnic. She complained about not being invited, to which 'Abd al-Ghani responded saying: "you have daughters and must stay with them." Tahira then said: "I, too, have my son 'Abd al-Rahman." 'Abd al-Ghani replied: "We shall take him with us, do not worry about him." Tahira died three days after her father, and her son shortly after. His son Isma'il was later stripped from the teaching posts he had inherited from his father and the light of the Nabulusis was thus eclipsed for good (*Wird*, 199).

In the many poetic eulogies written by 'Abd al-Ghani's followers and admirers, one described him eloquently as "the ocean of the law (*shari'a*), the pathway of the order (*tariqa*), the lamp of the truth (*haqiqa*): he was the steps for every high rising." (*Wird*, 208) Deeply saddened by the loss of his inspiring master, 'Abd al-Ghani's most illustrious disciple Mustafa al-Bakri wrote:

O Sun, why did you set on our land,
    and rise in the secure world.
The universe has darkened by your absence,
    as you proceeded to the auspicious home (*Tari*, 434).

AN ADVOCATE OF TRUTH

In 1676, the thirty-three-year-old Newton wrote a letter to his bitter enemy, Robert Hooke, which contained the much celebrated statement: "If I have seen farther, it is by standing on the shoulders of giants" (Hawking, 2002, ix). Standing on the shoulders of giants implied, among other things, a sense of continuity in achievements that enabled the rising to such a height that a whole new horizon of vision became possible. Yet it also implied a discontinuity with what those on the ground were confined to see. Thus on the shoulders of giants Newton was not only gazing at a new reality but was also looking in a new direction. Newton and many of his contemporaries became giants in their own right, on whose shoulders others stood to significantly transform the world, in good and bad ways, leading humanity to where it finds itself today.

At the age of thirty-three, 'Abd al-Ghani wrote a lengthy treatise in defence of Ibn 'Arabi, a Muslim giant on whose shoulders stood generations of eminent scholars and creative thinkers, including 'Abd al-Ghani himself. In the introduction, 'Abd al-Ghani was keen to explain that he was not defending the person but the truth found in his works. "Do not think that I am a zealous advocate of him," he wrote, "for I am a zealous advocate of the truth wherever it is" (*Matin*, 2). In his passionate pursuit of and unrelenting advocacy for the truth, 'Abd al-Ghani became a giant for many of his contemporaries. Many stood on his shoulders to reinforce the sense of continuity with tradition he zealously protected, despite his innovative, controversial, and often provocative views. But this continuity was suddenly ruptured when the following generations decided to abandon the shoulders of their predecessors and chose to mount the shoulders of the Europeans instead. Then, the great achievements of the scientific revolution and the Enlightenment were too alluring to be ignored, and the move carried a genuine promise to bring the Muslim and the European minds, experiences, and destinies closer to one another. But this was not to be. The experience of the Arab Awakening that was predicated on that of the Enlightenment failed to deliver on its promises, and two centuries later Islam and the West find themselves back in a medieval climate of animosity, conflict, and war.

In this destructive climate, and with the insights of the postmodern critique that provided new evaluation of the Enlightenment and modern rationalism, the rich, unexplored legacy of 'Abd al-Ghani offers constructive sites for rethinking of the intellectual interaction between Islam and the West. Three areas of his thought are particularly pertinent to today's problems: his philosophy of religion, his philosophy of being, and his unusual mix of rationality and mysticism. His thoughts in these areas have many limitations and problems of their own, of course, and promise no ready-made solutions; however, they offer alternative starting points to the ones currently engaged. His philosophy of religion offers a possibility of ecumenism anchored in Islamic religious thinking that is more conducive to constructive interactions between religions than the current sentiment, which is inspired by Wahhabism and the fundamentalist legacy of Ibn Taymiyya. His philosophy of being and especially his anti-Cartesian views resonate with the current Heideggerian critique that aims at breaking the rigid subject–object polarity and the Enlightenment rationalism that was constructed upon it. And his unusual mix of rationality and mysticism offers an opportunity to rediscover a place for the mysterious that the Enlightenment had entrusted science to eradicate. As Muslims have rarely considered their intellectual achievements and orientations during the Enlightenment, and Europeans were too blinded by their own positivism and rationalism to see the merits of anything else, 'Abd al-Ghani's legacy offers both a new focus and a new meeting place.

In their own historical context, outside the imposition of today's pressing issues, 'Abd al-Ghani's works offer historians and social scientists copious research material for future studies. First, his many legal studies that examine individual and social practices prevalent at the time, including corrupt government practices, are yet to be explored. Writing as an advocate of truth and social justice from outside the official hierarchy, his views shed valuable light on the sociopolitical climate of the period and especially the power dynamics between the Arabs and the Turks. Second, his commentaries on the works of the leading figures of his period and his intellectual exchanges with them, which were touched upon only briefly here, call for more detailed and profound examinations. This can shed new light on the intellectual developments of his period. Third, his correspondence with colleagues and followers in the region, and especially with the Turks, still await interested scholars. These exchanges, which include a treatise on the meanings of holy war (*jihad*) he sent to a close friend in Istanbul when the Ottoman army was facing defeat in Europe, can shed light on the shared interests and common concerns in the region. And fourth, his secular poetry, compiled in his anthology *The Wine of Babel*, presents interesting imageries of gender and urban entertainment in seventeenth- and eighteenth-century Damascus. It shows how feminine presence was entertained by men poetically in the physical absence of woman. The anthology is also a valuable record of the urban history of Damascus, presenting an image of the city's urbanity that was completely effaced by the rapid expansion and modernisation of the nineteenth and twentieth centuries.

With regard to his Sufism, 'Abd al-Ghani's personality presents an unconventional model of a scholar-mystic and an advocate of truth and social justice, one who is interested in the mundane affairs of the society while being able to guide his own mystical development and deliver his own spiritual attainments. To what extent this new complexion was a reflection of the changing nature and practices of Sufism at the time is a question that also calls for further studies. In such an inquiry, an important focus would be to see whether a new sense of Islamic humanism had evolved within the emerging complex web of intertwining rational and mystical thought. 'Abd al-Ghani, as we have seen in this brief study, gives some intriguing hints; his rich legacy offers much more:

> I am the substance, diffused without a diffusion,
>> I appear and disappear in all the truths.
> I am the centre of all turnings, for to my way
>> returns the order of all other ways.
> I am the outward, known in every status;
>> I am the inward, concealed among the creatures.
> I am: the Pole is my door keeper; I am: the Sustainer is my servant;
>> I am: the individual fears entering my straits.
> I am the light, the light of the eye; from me are constituted
>> all creatures, be they the longing or the longed for.
> I am knowledge, the knowledge of the Real in every being;
>> none understands my words except those who are able to taste
>> (Diwan, 343).

BIOGRAPHICAL SOURCES

In addition to 'Abd al-Ghani's own copious autobiographical notes, there are several primary and secondary sources on his life and works. The following is a brief introduction to the three key sources: the most reliable, the most comprehensive, and the most popular. Only the third source is available in a published form.

THE MOST RELIABLE

The Wholesome Drinking (al-Mashrab al-Hani) is a biographical account written by Hussein bin Tu'ma al-Baytamani (d. 1761), one of 'Abd al-Ghani's closest disciples. Despite its many shortcomings, it is the most reliable source. It was written in 1730 during 'Abd al-Ghani's life, about ten months before his death. Al-Baytamani was urged to write it by other fellow disciples who must have been concerned about the growing frailty of their beloved master and were anticipating his death. Al-Baytamani, though extremely passionate about his master, was not the brightest or the most inspired of his students. In fact, in his account, al-Baytamani tries to defend himself against a claim of lack of intelligence, explaining that if he sometimes appeared distracted or sleepy during the lessons it was because of his intense concentration in order to absorb his master's profound teachings. Although the quality of his text may lend credence to the claim, his loyalty, attachment, and devotion to his master could not be questioned. These were reflected clearly in the text, making it an unmediated, simple, and honest recount of the master's life. It is unlikely that 'Abd al-Ghani, in his last days at the age of ninety-two, would have had the desire to check the text, but it would certainly have been carefully read and checked by al-Baytamani's fellow disciples. Lengthy and detailed as it is, the most important aspect of this source is the lack of explicit reference to 'Abd al-Ghani's lengthy spiritual retreat that is often presented to be a defining period in the master's life and spiritual experience.

THE MOST COMPREHENSIVE

The Intimate Invocation (al-Wird al-Unsi) is a biographical account written by 'Abd al-Ghani's nephew, Kamal al-Din al-Ghazzi (d. 1799). This is by far the most comprehensive, structured, detailed, and indeed useful source. It is extensive and sophisticated, giving copious details not only on 'Abd al-Ghani's life, works, and visionary experiences, but also on the genealogy of his family, on his teachers, and on the wide circle of his disciples. The main problem with this source, however, is its carefully constructed nature when compared with the spontaneous text of al-Baytamani. Al-Ghazzi was clearly basking in the glory of his family that had already exhausted its precious human resources and produced its last shining star. He was careful to construct a stereotypical image of an inspiring and inspired great Sufi master, one who at a mature point in life (forty years of age, after the example of the Prophet), enters his private retreat, reflects and contemplates, receives dazzling revelations, and then emerges as an enlightened saint. He divided 'Abd al-Ghani's life neatly into three main stages: growth, seclusion, and authority.

1. Growth, the first forty years (1050–1090 / 1641–1680)
2. Seclusion, seven years, (1091–1098 / 1681–1687)
3. Authority, forty-six years, (1098–1143 / 1687–1731)

Al-Ghazzi's construction has been accepted at face value by most researchers working on 'Abd al-Ghani. A critical cross-examination of this source, however, reveals elements of inaccuracy and contrivance in its representations. 'Abd al-Ghani's eccentric and colourful personality seems too complex to fit in such a conventional model. Al-Ghazzi referred to, consulted, and, to some degree, was influenced by al-Baytamani's account. Both texts share a curious feature: they quote in full a single text of mystical reflections by 'Abd al-Ghani, parts of which are presented in the form of a dialogue between God and 'Abd al-Ghani. In this, al-Ghazzi follows al-Baytamani and seems eager to emphasize the profundity of 'Abd al-Ghani's knowledge and the authenticity of his mystical experience.

THE MOST POPULAR

The Threading of Pearls (*Salk al-Durar*) is an acclaimed biographical dictionary, which includes an extended entry on 'Abd al-Ghani by the eminent Damascene scholar Khalil al-Muradi (d. 1791). Unlike the two previous humble authors, al-Muradi was Damascus' Chief Jurisconsult (*mufti*) of the Hanafi school, the post 'Abd al-Ghani assumed briefly later on in his career, and Head of the Damascene Nobles. He was also related to 'Abd al-Ghani: his paternal uncle was married to the daughter of 'Abd al-Ghani's son, Isma'il. Al-Muradi was a friend and a relative of al-Ghazzi, and both must have exchanged notes on their eminent relative. It is not clear whose account was written first as both refer to each other's texts. It is likely that both were written about the same time as both concur in their differences from al-Baytamani's. Being merely a short entry in a biographical dictionary, al-Muradi's biography is very brief compared with the other two accounts, with much space being devoted to the listing of 'Abd al-Ghani's works. Being published and widely accessible, however, it is the most widely quoted text by the general researchers and editors of 'Abd al-Ghani's works.

SELECTED BIBLIOGRAPHY

LIST OF MANUSCRIPTS CITED

AE.: 'Atif Efendi Library, Istanbul.

Kan.: Kandilli Observatory Library, Istanbul.

Prin.: Princeton University Library, Yahuda Section, Garrett Collection, Princeton.

Top.: Topkapi Saray Library, Istanbul.

Zah.: Zahiriyya Library listing, Maktabat al-Asad, Damascus.

Al-Baytamani, Hussein b. Tu'ma. Prin. MS 1808. *Al-Mashrab al-Hani fi Tarjamat al-'Arif Sidi 'Abd al-Ghani.*

Al-Dimashqi, Abu Bakr b. Bihram. Top. MS 325. *Kitab Nusrat al-Islam wa al-Surur fi Tahrir Kitab Atlas Mayur.*

Al-Ghazzi, Kamal al-Din. Zah. MS 281. *Al-Wird al-Unsi wa al-Warid al-Qudsi fi Tarjamat al-Shaykh 'Abd al-Ghani al-Nabulusi.*

Ibn 'Arabi, Muhyi al-Din. Zah. MS 8376. *Al-Shajara al-Nu'maniyya al-Kubra fi al-Dawla al-'Uthmaniyya wa ma Yata'allaq bi-Muddatiha min al-Hawadith al-Kawniyya.*

Kemal Pashazade. AE. MS 2851/21. *Risala fi Haqiqat al-Insan.*

Köse Ibrahim. Kan. MS 403. *Secencelü'l-Eflak fi Gayeti 'l-Idrak.*

Al-Nabulusi, 'Abd al-Ghani. Zah. MS 9868. *Bawatin al-Qur'an wa Mawatin al-Furqan.*

———. Zah. MS 6979. *Burhan al-Thubut fi Tabri'at Harut wa Marut.*

———. Zah. MS 1407. *Al-Hadiqa al-Nadiyya Sharh al-Tariqa al-Muhammadiyya.*

———. Zah. MS 14123. *Jawab 'ala Su'al Warad min Taraf al-Nasara.*

———. Zah. MS 1502. *Jawhir al-Nusus fi Hall Kalimat al-Fusus.*

———. Zah. MS 111. *Kashf al-Bayan 'an Asrar al-Adyan.*

———. Prin. MS 295. *Al-Kawkab al-Mutalali fi Sharh Qasidat al-Ghazali.*

———. Prin. MS 295. *Miftah al-Futuh fi Mishkat al-Jism wa Zujajat al-Nafs wa Misbah al-Ruh.*

———. Zah. MS 733. *Munajat al-Hakim wa Munaghat al-Qadim.*

———. Zah. MS 6979. *Radd al-Jahil ila al-Sawab fi Jawaz Idafat al-Ta'thir ila al-Asbab.*

———. Zah. MS 1418. *Al-Radd 'ala man Takallam fi Ibn al-'Arabi.*

———. Zah. MS 11087. *Miftah al-Ma'iyya Sharh Tariq al-Naqshbandiyya.*

———. Prin. MS 295. *Radd al-Muftari 'an al-Ta'n bi al-Shushtari.*

———. Zah. MS 9873. *Al-Radd al-Matin 'ala Muntaqis al-'Arif Muhyi al-Din.*

———. Zah. MS 17861. *Radd al-Ta'nif 'ala al-Mu'annif wa Ithbat Jahl haza al-Musannif.*

———. Zah. MS 14123. *Risala fi al-'Aqa'id al-Islamiyya.*

———. Zah. MS 6078. *Tahrik Silsilat al-Widad fi Mas'alat Khalq Af'al al-'Ibad.*

———. Zah. MS 6979. *Takmil al-Nu'ut fi Luzum al-Buyut.*

———. Zah. MS 6979. *'Uzr al-A'imma fi Nush al-Umma.*

Al-Siddiqi, Mustafa Bakri. Zah. MS 5316. *Al-Fath al-Tari al-Jani fi ba'd Ma'athir 'Abd al-Ghani.*

PRIMARY ARABIC SOURCES CITED

Al-Dawani, Jalal al-Din. 1953. *Shawakil al-Hur fi Sharh Hayakil al-Nur.* Madras: Government Oriental Manuscripts Library, reprint Dar Biblion.

Al-Ghazali, Abi Hamid. nd. *Al-Mustasfa min 'Ilm al-Usul.* Beirut: Dar al-Fikr, 2 vols.

Al-Ghazzi, Najm al-Din. 1997. *Al-Kawakib al-Sa'ira bi-A'yan al-Ma'a al-'Ashira.* Beirut: Dar al-Kutub al-'Ilmiyya, 3 vols.

Hajji Khalifa, Mustafa b. 'Abd Allah. 1835. *Kashf al-Zunun 'an Asami al-Kutub wa al-Funun.* London: R. Benttey, Dar Sadir reprint, 7 vols.

Ibn 'Arabi, Muhyi al-Din. 1980. *Fusus al-Hikam.* Beirut: Dar al-Kitab al-'Arabi.

———. 1978. *Tarjuman al-Ashwaq.* London: Theosophical Publishing House.

Ibn Kinnan al-Salihi. 1992. *Al-Mawakib Al-Islamiyya fi al-Mamalik wa al-Mahasin al-Shamiyya.* Damascus: Wazarat al-Thaqafa, 2 vols.

Ibn Tulun, Muhammad. nd. *Al-Qala'id al-Jawhariyya fi Tarikh al-Salihiyya.* Damascus: Majma' al-Lugha al-'Arabiyya, 2 vols.

Al-Khiyari, Ibrahim. 1969. *Tuhfat al-Udaba' wa Salwat al-Ghuraba'.* Baghdad: Dar al-Jumhuriyya, 2 vols.

Al-Muhibbi, Muhammad. nd. *Khulasat al-Athar fi A'yan al-Qarn al-Hadi 'Ashar*. Beirut: Dar Sadir, 4 vols.

Al-Muradi, Abi al-Fadl. 1997. *Salk al-Durar fi A'yan al-Qarn al-Thani 'Ashar*. Beirut: Dar al-Kutub al-'Ilmiyya, 4 vols.

Al-Nabulusi, 'Abd al-Ghani. 2001. *Al-Ajwiba 'ala Wahid wa Sittun Su'al*. Damascus: Dar al-Farabi.

———.2001. *Al-Fath al-Rabbani wa al-Fayd al-Rahmani*. Beirut: Dar al-Kutub al-'Ilmiyya.

———. 1999. *Khamrat al-Han wa Rannat al-Alhan*. Damascus: Dar Qutayba.

———. 1998. *Dhakha'ir al-Mawarith fi al-Dalala 'ala Mawadi' al-Ahadith*. Beirut: Dar al-Kutub al-'Ilmiyya, 2 vols.

———. 1998. *Al-Haqiqa wa al-Majaz fi Rihalt Bilad al-Sham wa Misr wa al-Hijaz*. Damascus: Dar al-Ma'rifa.

———. 1998. *Ta'tir al-Anam fi Ta'bir al-Manam*. Beirut: Dar al-Ma'rifa.

———. 1995. *Al-Wujud al-Haqq wa al-Khitab al-Sidqq*. Damascus: Institut Français de Arab.

———. 1990. *Al-Hadra al-Unsiyya fi al-Rihla al-Qudsiyya*. Beirut: al-Masadir.

———.1988. *Khamrat Babel wa Shaduw al-Balabel*. Damascus: Dar al-Ma'rifa.

———. 1986. *Diwan al-Haqa'iq wa Majmu' al-Raqa'iq*. Beirut: Dar al-Jil.

———. 1986. *Al-Lu'lu' al-Maknun fi Hukm al-Ikhbar 'amma Sayakun*. Beirut: Dar al-Kutub al-'Ilmiyya.

———. 1984. *Nafahat al-Azhar 'ala Nasamat al-Ashar*. Beirut: 'Alam al-Kutub.

Al-Shahrastani, Abi al-Fath. 1984. *Al-Milal wa al-Nihal*. Beirut: Dar al-Ma'rifa.

Al-Suhrawardi, Shihab al-Din. 2005. *Hayakil al-Nur*. Paris: Dar Biblion.

Tashkubrizade, Ahmad b. Mustafa. 2002. *Miftah al-Sa'ada wa Misbah al-Siyada fi Maudu'at al-'Ulum*. Beirut: Dar al-Kutub al-'Ilmiyya, 3rd ed.

SECONDARY SOURCES AND FURTHER READING

Akkach, Samer. 2005a. *Cosmology and Architecture in Premodern Islam: An Architectural Reading of Mystical Ideas*. Albany: State University of New York Press.

———. 2005b. "The Poetics of Concealment: Al-Nabulusi's Encounter with the Dome of the Rock." *Muqarnas* 22: 110-27.

———. 2002. "Mapping Difference: On the Islamic Concept of *Fada'il.*" In S. Akkach, ed., *De-Placing Difference: Architecture, Culture and Imaginative Geography*. Adelaide: Centre for Asian and Middle Eastern Architecture.

Alddin, Bakri. 1985. "'Abdalgani an-Nabulusi (1143/1731): Oeuvre, vie et doctrine." PhD dissertation. Paris: Université de Paris I, 2 vols.

Anscombe, Elizabeth and Peter T. Geach. 1954. *Descartes: Philosophical Writings*. Middlesex: Thomas Nelson.

Barbir, Karl. 1980. *Ottoman Rule in Damascus, 1708–1758*. Princeton: Princeton University Press.

Barnett, S. J. 2003. *The Enlightenment and Religion: The Myths of Modernity*. Manchester: Manchester University Press.

Bergin, Joseph, ed. 2001. *The Seventeenth Century: Europe 1598–1715*. Oxford: Oxford University Press.

Black, Jeremy. 1999. *Eighteenth-Century Europe*. London: Macmillan, 2nd ed.

Blanning, T. C. W., ed. 2000. *The Eighteenth Century: Europe 1688–1815*. Oxford: Oxford University Press.

Brooke, John Hedley. 1991. *Science and Religion: Some Historical Perspectives*. Cambridge: Cambridge University Press.

Cachia, Pierre. 1998. *The Arch Rhetorician* or *The Schemer's Skimmer: a Handbook of Late Arabic badi'*. Wiesbaden: Harrassowitz.

Degeorge, Gérard. 2004. *Damascus*. Paris: Flammarion.

Dupré, Louis. 2004. *The Enlightenment and the Intellectual Foundations of Modern Culture*. New Haven and London: Yale University Press.

Fara, Patricia. 2002. *Newton: The Making of Genius*. London: Macmillan.

Gran, Peter. 1998. *Islamic Roots of Capitalism*. Syracuse: Syracuse University Press.

Hagen, Gottfried and Tilman Seidensticker. 1998. "Reinhard Schulzes Hypothese einer islamischen Aufklärung." *Zeitschrift der Deutschen Morgenländischen Gesellschaft* 148: 83–110.

Hawking, Stephen, ed., *On the Shoulders of Giants: The Great Works of Physics and Astronomy*. Philadelphia and London: Running Press.

Heinen, Anton. 1982. *Islamic Cosmology*. Beirut: Orient-Institut.

Horkheimer, Max and Theodor Adorno. 1973. *Dialectic of Enlightenment*. London: Allen Lane.

Hourani, Albert. 1991. *A History of the Arab Peoples*. New York: MJF Books.

Howard, Deborah. 2000. *Venice and the East: the Impact of the Islamic World on Venetian Architecture 1100–1500*. New Haven: Yale University Press.

Huff, Toby E. 1993. *The Rise of Early Modern Science: Islam, China and the West*. Cambridge: Cambridge University Press.

Hyland, Paul, Olga Gomez and Francesca Greensides. 2003. *The Enlightenment: A Sourcebook and Reader*. London: Routledge.

Ihsanoğlu, Ekmeleddin. 2004. *Science, Technology and Learning in the Ottoman Empire*. Hampshire: Ashgate.

Israel, Jonathan. 2001. *Radical Enlightenment*. Oxford: Oxford University Press.

Knysh, Alexander. 1999. *Ibn 'Arabi in the Later Islamic Tradition: The Making of a Polemical Image in Medieval Islam*. Albany: State University of New York Press.

Levtzion, Nehemia and John Voll, eds. 1987. *Eighteenth-Century Renewal and Reform in Islam*. New York: Syracuse University Press.

Makdisi, George. 1981. *The Rise of Colleges: Institutions of Learning in Islam and the West*. Edinburgh: Edinburgh University Press.

McGrane, Bernard. 1989. *Beyond Anthropology: Society and the Other*. New York: Columbia University Press.

Melton, James Van Horn. 2001. *The Rise of the Public in Enlightenment Europe*. Cambridge: Cambridge University Press.

Radtke, Bernd. 2000. *Autochthone islamische Aufklärung in 18 Jahrhundert*. Utrecht: Houtsma Stichting.

Robinson, Francis. 1997. "Ottoman-Safavids-Mughals: Shared Knowledge and Connective Systems." *Journal of Islamic Studies* 8, 2: 151–184.

El-Rouayheb, Khaled. 2006. "Opening the Gate of Verification: The Forgotten Arab-Islamic Florescence of the 17th Century." *International Journal of Middle Eastern Studies* 38: 263–281.

Saliba, George. 1999. "Whose Science is Arabic Science in Renaissance Europe?" http://www.columbia.edu/~gas1/project/visions/case1.html. Columbia University.

———. 1994. *A History of Arabic Astronomy: Planetary Theories during the Golden Age of Islam*. Albany: State University of New York Press.

Sayili, Aydin. 1960. *The Observatory in Islam*. Ankara: Turk Tarih Kurumu Basimevi.

Schulze, Reinhard. 1996. "Was ist die islamische Aufklarung?" *Die Welt des Islams* 36: 276–325.

Shaw, Stanford. 1976. *History of the Ottoman Empire and Modern Turkey. Volume I: Empire of the Gazis: The Rise and Decline of the Ottoman Empire, 1280–1808.* Cambridge: Cambridge University Press.

Sirriyeh, Elizabeth. 2005. *Sufi Visionary of Ottoman Damascus: 'Abd al-Ghani al-Nabulusi, 1641–1731.* London and New York: Routledge Curzon.

———. 2001. "Whatever Happened to Banu Jama'a? The Tale of a Scholarly Family in Ottoman Syria." *British Journal of Middle Eastern Studies* 28, 1: 55–56.

———. 1999. *Sufis and Anti-Sufis: The Defence, Rethinking and Rejection of Sufism in the Modern World.* Richmond: Cruzon.

———. 1985. "The Mystical Journeys of 'Abd al-Ghani al-Nabulusi." *Die Welt des Islams* 25: 84–96.

———. 1979. "The Journeys of 'Abd al-Ghani al-Nabulusi in Palastine." *Journal of Semitic Studies* 24, 1: 55–69.

———. 1979. "*Ziyarat* of Syria in a Rihla of 'Abd al-Ghani al-Nabulusi (1050/1641–1143/1731)." *Journal of the Royal Asiatic Society:* 109–122.

Voll, John. 1999. "Foundations for Renewal and Reform: Islamic Movements in the Eighteenth and Nineteenth Centuries." In John Esposito, ed., *The Oxford History of Islam.* Oxford: Oxford University Press, 509–547.

———. 1975. "Old 'Ulama' Families and Ottoman Influence in Eighteenth Century Damascus." *American Journal of Arabic Studies* 3: 48–59.

Von Schlegell, Barbara. 1997. "Sufism in the Ottoman Arab World: Shaykh 'Abd al-Ghani al-Nabulusi (d. 1143/1731)." PhD dissertation. Berkeley: University of California.

Winter, Michael. 1988. "A Polemical Treatise by 'Abd al-Ghani al-Nabulusi against a Turkish Scholar on the Religious Status of the *dhimmis.*" *Arabica* 35: 92–103.

Yahya, 'Uthman. 2001. *Mu'allafat Ibn 'Arabi: Tarikhuha wa Tasnifuha.* Cairo: al-Hay'a al-Misriyya al-'Amma li al-Kitab.

Zilfi, Madeline. 1986. "The Kadizadelis: Discordant Revivalism in Seventeenth-Century Istanbul." *Journal of Near Eastern Studies* 45, 4: 251–269.

INDEX

'Abd al-Ghani al-Nabulusi 6–7; birth 10;
inspired by Ibn 'Arabi 11, 109,
133–4; lineage 20–4; childhood and
youth 25; goes to Istanbul 27–30;
teachers of 33–4; reading 34–5; in
retreat 36, 37–8 39; ill-treatment of
36–7; travels 39–43; reputation of
40, 131; argument with Governor of
Damascus 52; and Arabic language
118–19; lifestyle and personality
126–7, 136; moves to al-Salihiyya
129–30; later life 131; pavilion
131; death 131; family of 132–3;
eulogies 133; as an advocate for
truth 133–6; **thought** xii, 35,
127, 134–5; on Christianity 117,
118; dialogue with God 91–2, 126,
127; and divine permission 85–7;
ecumenism 107, 112, 114, 116,
134; public readings of mystical texts
123–6; and self-consciousness 99,
100–3; and Sufism xii, 6–7, 25–6,
29, 30, 31–2, 34, 107–8, 127, 136;
truth and law polarity 108–11,
113–14; and Unity of Being 89–94,
108, 112, 131; **works** 6, 35, 45–6,
127, 135; *The Anthology of Truths* 46;
*Clarifying the Intent in the Meaning of
the Unity of Being* 89; commentaries
34, 35, 39, 47–8, 90, 101, 106, 116,
129–30, 131, 135; *The Concealed
Pearls...* 57–8; *Conversing with the
Wise...* 91–4; *The Disclosure and
Clarification of the Secrets of Religions*
111–14; *The Evening Breezes...* 27;
The Firm Statement in Clarifying the
Knowers' Belief in Unity 90, 131; *The
Flowers' Fragrances on the Evening
Breezes* 27; *The Glittering Planet* 101;
hadith index 48–51; *The Imams'
Excuse in Guiding the Community* 111;
The Inner Meanings of the Qur'an...
39; *The Key of Openings...* 98, 101,
102; *The Key of Togetherness in
Expounding the Naqshbandiyya* 31; *The
Lordly Opening...* 109; *The
Muhammadan Way* 39; *Nafahat...* 27;
*Perfecting the Attributes in Remaining at
Home* 34; poetry 17–18, 26–7,
135; *The Real Being and Truthful
Discourse* 89–90; *A Response to the
One who Spoke about Ibn al-'Arabi*
118–19; *Returning the Ignorant to the
Right...* 87–8; travel memoirs
40–3; *the Treasures of Heritage...*
48–51; *A Treatise Concerning Man*
101; *A Treatise on the Islamic
Doctrines* 30, 108–9; *The
Understandings of the Unseen* 89;
The Wine of Babel... 46, 122, 135;
The Wine of Longing... 89, 109, 110
'Abd al-Rahman Efendi 27
Adrianople (Edirne) 12
Ahmed III, Sultan 74
'Ajlan family 19
Alembert, Jean d' 60
Alfonso X, King of Spain 71
Anatolia 12
anthropology 62, 104, 105
anti-Sufi movement 29, 35, 40, 79, 106
Arabic language 13, 52, 118–19
Arislan, shaykh 109, 110

147

ethnicity 118, 119
Europe (*see also* Enlightenment):
    colonization by 62; Muslim
    interaction with 71–2, 74–5, 106,
    134; scientific worldview 4;
    secularisation of society 119–20;
    warfare in 62

faith: natural 117; reason and 52–3, 58,
    60, 61, 63; and unbelief 117–18
Fayd Allah, Shaykh al-Islam 106
France, Enlightenment in 60–1
Franklin, Benjamin 63
free will 82, 83, 114

Gadamer, Hans-Georg 103
Galileo, Galilei 61, 64
geocentric universe 54, 74, 75, 93, 94
geography 53, 71, 72, 74
al-Ghazali 76
al-Ghazzi, Badr al-Din 22
al-Ghazzi, Kamal al-Din, biography of
    'Abd al-Ghani 10, 38, 39, 40, 131,
    138–9
al-Ghazzi, Najm al-Din 25, 33
Gibbon, Edward 65
God 79, 112, 114–15; Ash'ariyya and
    83; as Being 89–90, 91–2; and
    guidance/misguidance 115;
    Mu'tazila and 82–3; power of 80,
    82, 87, 88, 93; scientists and 80;
    and self 102
Grotius, Hugo 61

hadith 49; 'Abd al-Ghani studied 33;
    index of 48–9, 50–1
Hajji Khalifa 5, 53, 57, 74, 75–6, 106;
    awareness of Europe 71; *Cihannüma*
    74; *Clarifying the Uncertainties* 72,
    76–8
Halley's comet 55
Hama 29
Hamza family 19
Hanafi law 18, 23–4, 33

al-Hanbali, Ibn al-'Imad 72
Haqqi, Ibrahim 53, 75
Heidegger, Martin 103
heliocentric universe 54, 64, 67, 68–9,
    75, 94
al-Hindi, Fadl Allah 90, 131
Hobbes, Thomas 61, 95
Holbach, Baron d' 66
holy war (*jihad*) 135
human nature 94–5; Descartes and
    96–7
Hume, David 94

I *see* ego
Ibn 'Arabi 10–12, 31, 35, 112, 116;
    influence on 'Abd al-Ghani 11, 109,
    133–4; and love 113; public
    readings of works of 123–4; and
    suffering 117–18; Sultan Selim and
    15–16; and Unity of Being 85, 89,
    92, 93
Ibn Badr 33
Ibn Khaldun 76
Ibn Kinnan 16
Ibn Sab'in 116
Ibn al-Shatir 67
Ibn Taymiyya 134
Ibn Tulun 21
ignorance 66, 78, 105
'Imadi family 19
inertia, Newton and 93
infidelity 105, 117–18
inspiration, 'Abd al-Ghani's sources of
    45–6
intellectual exchanges: with Europe
    106, 134; in public 122–3, 124–5,
    135
Islam 12, 113; rationalism in 82–4;
    religious authority 104–5; rise of
    extremism 106; and science 67–79;
    superiority of 106, 111, 115, 116,
    117; universality of 116–17; and the
    West 134–5
Islamic enlightenment xi, 3, 4, 5–6, 48